The
Good
Atheist

The
Good
Atheist

Living a Purpose-Filled Life Without God

Dan Barker

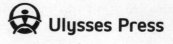 Ulysses Press

Published in the U.S. by
ULYSSES PRESS
P.O. Box 3440
Berkeley, CA 94703
www.ulyssespress.com

ISBN13: 978-1-56975-846-5
Library of Congress Control Number 2010925858

Acquisitions Editor: Keith Riegert
Managing Editor: Claire Chun
Editor: Richard Harris
Editorial Associates: Lauren Harrison
Cover design: what!design @ whatweb.com
Cover photos: tree background © istockphoto.com/Camrocker;
    tree © istockphoto.com/Coldimages; grass © istockphoto.
    com/kutaytanir; seedling © istockphoto.com/craftvision;
    clouds © istockphoto.com/Viorika; stationery paper ©
    istockphoto.com/billnoll
Production: Judith Metzener

Printed in Canada by Webcom

10 9 8 7 6 5 4 3 2 1

Distributed by Publishers Group West

PURPOSE DRIVEN is a registered trademark of Richard D. Warren
and is used here for purpose of commentary and criticism only.
This book is independently authored and published and is not
sponsored or endorsed by, or affiliated in any way with, Richard
D. Warren.

Table of Contents

Foreword

I WISH I HAD HAD THIS BOOK to read when I was going through my struggles with faith. Back then, I knew that the arguments for god were weak, but I wasn't sure where to begin making sense of life without god. It took years of reading and thinking to spin my way out. I'm still spinning my way out, and just reading this book helped me organize my thoughts—things I already knew and understood seem clearer and more grounded. I appreciate that Dan has taken the time and done the research to write this book. I bet you're going to love reading it.

Letting go of faith and accepting that I'm a free agent able to make choices, find purpose, and take action based on my own personal desires and my own personal volition was ultimately liberating. Years of religious instruction and indoctrination were hard to undo. Life was easier with prescribed choices and a premade list of what was right and wrong. On the other hand, living without god—or some divinely inspired purpose—can be scary as well. It's hard to make complicated choices. And not all the choices we make lead to the outcomes we wish for. Sometimes what we wish for isn't what we want anyway!

When you're religious, there's always an answer that blunts the edge off anything catastrophic, or that guides you along, lulling you into a state of babyish calm when things are going well. But real life isn't like that. There are real catastrophes. There are real unfortunate outcomes. There are also real successes and real serendipitous joyful accidents—coincidences and hard work that pays off with more than we ever expected. That's life.

I love when Dan writes, "Life doesn't need purpose, purpose needs life." That is so true. I understand this to be the directed energy that a person—alive, cognizant, and with purpose—can bring to affect him or herself and the world.

Our consciousness is like having been given—by evolution—a kind of car. To me it's like a Ferrari that can go really fast and is very powerful. However, the religious are taught that their mind is more like a train car that needs an engine to pull it along. Without the engine at the front of the train, the car is stranded, and off the tracks it can't go anywhere.

But that's not true. Our minds have tremendous power. We can behave with great insight and discipline and compassion. Dan's book explains all those myths that the church and the religious keep on promoting—even when they've been shown to be wrong over and over again. The religious do this because they need believers in order to stay in power. Also, people gravitate toward this ideology because, in the short run, faith is comforting and easier. But in the long run, it is very costly.

I feel I am a much better citizen of my community, world, and family because I no longer believe in god. I make decisions on my own. It's often difficult, and I am often not always in lock-step with the thinking of others. But in general I do less harm, I am more compassionate, I use actions instead of intentions (or prayer), and I am generally tougher and more resilient without god in my life. I still get sad, I still make mistakes, I still brood and I still get depressed from time to time. But now I'm not grasping at supernatural concepts, or fuzzily-thought-out, half-baked, new-agey woo-woo. I rely on evidence, and I have an understanding of what makes for good evidence.

This book will be shocking and powerful if you're still making the transition out of religious belief, and it will be a great reminder of why you have confidence in your world-view if you're already a nonbeliever. I loved Dan's earlier books, *Losing Faith in Faith* and *Godless*. With this book, Dan goes further and deeper. He has matured in his thinking just as I am trying to do the same. He's made it all much easier for me.

So ... enjoy.

Julia Sweeney

Preface

WHEN I REJECTED CHRISTIANITY in 1983 after 19 years of preaching, my self-excision was traumatically painful. My commitment to Jesus had given me a source of purpose, destiny, and fulfillment. Ordained to the ministry, I had been an associate pastor in three California churches. I also spent years trekking across Mexico in missionary work—small villages, jungles, deserts, large arenas, radio, television, parks, prisons, and street meetings. I spent more years in traveling evangelism across the United States, preaching and singing wherever audiences could be found—churches, street corners, house-to-house witnessing, and college campuses. I wrote many worshipful Christian songs and musicals, some of which are still being performed today.

I did not lose my faith. I gave it up purposely. The motivation that drove me into the ministry was the same that drove me out. I have always wanted to know. Even as a child I had fervently pursued truth. I was rarely content to accept things without examination, and my examinations were intense. I was a thirsty learner, a good student, and a good minister because of that drive.

Since I was taught and believed Christianity was the answer, the only hope for "man," I dedicated myself to understanding all I possibly could. I devoured every book, every sermon, and the bible. I prayed, fasted, and obeyed biblical teaching. I decided that I would lean my whole weight upon the truth of scripture. This attitude, I am sure, gave the impression that I could be trusted as a Christian authority and leader. Christians, eager for substantiation, gladly allowed me to assume a place of leadership, and I took it as confirmation of my holy calling.

For years I went through an intense inner conflict. On the one hand I was happy with the direction and fulfillment of my Christian life; on the other hand I had intellectual doubts. Faith and reason began a war within me. And it kept escalating. I would cry out to God for answers, and none would come. Like the battered wife who clings to hope, I kept trusting that God would someday come through. He never did.

I finally realized that faith is a cop-out, a defeat, an admission that the truths of religion are unknowable through evidence and reason. It is only undemonstrable assertions that require the suspension of reason, and weak ideas that require faith. I just lost faith in faith. Biblical contradictions became more and more discrepant, apologist arguments more and more absurd, and, when I finally discarded faith, things became more and more clear.

It was like tearing my whole frame of reality to pieces, ripping to shreds the fabric of meaning and hope, betraying the values of existence. It was like spitting on my mother, or like throwing one of my children out a window. It was sacrilege. All of my bases for thinking and values had to be restructured.

There was no specific turning point for me. I one day just realized that I was no longer a Christian. Yet I was a preacher for many years, and I guess it hasn't all rubbed off. I would wish to influence others who may be struggling like I did, to influence them to have the guts to think. To think deliberately and clearly. To take no fact without critical examination and to remain open to honest inquiry, wherever it leads.

I shared the story of my journey from evangelical preacher to atheist spokesperson in much greater detail in an earlier book, *Godless* (Berkeley: Ulysses Press, 2008). In that journey, I've found that one of the greatest challenges facing "post-Christian" converts after their departure from their churches is that because atheism has no church, no cult, no creed, no dogma (nor do we want or need such things) many nonbelievers feel alone, lacking an opportunity to sit and discuss practical answers to life's little problems—and big ones. The kind that haunt you at four in the morning, when you're lying awake wondering whether you've made the correct choices in life. Questions like, "Since God doesn't exist, what am I here for?"

The purpose of this book is purpose itself. I will show you how most non-believers I know deal with the question: "What is the purpose of life?" I will also introduce you to many other atheists, agnostics, and freethinkers of every stripe who have discovered the truly good news that we don't need a god to tell us how to live. Since your life is the only thing you truly own, how *you* choose to live it is what gives it purpose.

PART 1

Life-Driven
Purpose

AROUND THE SAME TIME I severed my ties with Christianity, a new face appeared on the evangelical scene. Rick Warren, a young Baptist minister by training, conducted the first service of Saddleback Church in a middle school gymnasium in Laguna Hills, California. Two hundred people attended.

I didn't pay much attention to Pastor Warren or his church at the time. I probably never heard his name mentioned. Did the world really need another ultra-conservative preacher to rail against such societal evils as abortion, gay rights, and the perils of atheism? I, for one, certainly did not.

I first took notice of Rick Warren a decade or so later. Saddleback Church had expanded into larger quarters—specifically, a large plastic tent with seating for 2,300 people at a time. Soon after, Warren rocketed into national prominence with the publication of his book, *The Purpose Driven™ Life: What on Earth Am I Here For?* It quickly became one of the best-selling books of the 20th century. Somehow, I didn't get around to reading it.

But Warren's profile kept getting higher. His church grew to become one of the largest in the United States. His hulking, goateed, twinkle-eyed, Texas-drawled presence started popping up everywhere—the Harvard School of Government,

17

the Council on Foreign Relations, and the United Nations, to name a few. *US News and World Report* listed him among "America's 25 Top Leaders"; *Newsweek* ranked him as one of the "15 People Who Made America Great"; and *Time* magazine dubbed him one of the "15 World Leaders Who Mattered Most in 2004" and, the following year, one of the "100 Most Influential People in the World." When he was selected to moderate the 2008 presidential candidates' televised debate on religion and then to deliver the invocation at President Obama's inauguration, I decided it was high time I found out what this guy was about.

So I finally read his book—and I was appalled.

Never mind that it is filled with misleading quotes out of context and tortured interpretations of verses picked and chosen from no fewer than 15 different translations of the bible. Never mind that it completely overlooks a few matters such as the crucifixion, resurrection, and ascension—central events in the New Testament, at least back in my Christian days. As I read on, it slowly dawned on me that *The Purpose Driven*™ *Life* is all about promoting *slavery*.

"It's not about you," Warren confidently informs us. You have no say in your own purpose. Falling under the spell of the bible and the myth of a supernatural creator, Rick Warren claims to know that a god scripted your role before you were born. "His purpose for your life predates your conception," Warren says. "He planned it before you existed, without your input! You may choose your career, your spouse, your hobbies, and many other parts of your life, but you don't get to choose your purpose." And what exactly is the purpose of life, according to Warren's book? It is to worship God, find fellowship with Christians, become like Christ, serve others, and evangelize. That's it! You were born so that you can go to church and convince others to join you.

"If you want to know why you were placed on this planet," Warren assures us, "you must begin with God. You were born *by* his purpose and *for* his purpose."

It follows that those of us who do not hold Warren's beliefs lead empty lives: "Without God, life has no purpose, and without purpose, life has no meaning. Without meaning, life has no significance or hope." Apparently, Rev. Warren hasn't met many atheists. He seems forgetful or unaware of the fact that hundreds of millions of good people on this planet do not "begin with God," do not believe in a god, yet live happy, moral, hopeful, loving, meaningful, productive, purpose-filled lives. Has Warren ever talked with any of us good atheists? We don't think we are the ones with the problem. We know we are alive. We think it is sad that so many Christians pretend to have no purpose of their own, that they must bow as servants before someone else's plan for their lives, especially before a mythical slave master!

If you need a purpose-driven life, you are an actor in someone else's play. You are following a script, and it's not even a good one. If your life only has meaning while it is being directed in someone else's movie, you have no life of your own. You have been subjugated, cheated, and robbed. We atheists think you deserve better. You should emancipate yourself and reclaim your rightful property.

A Slave by Any Other Name

Like Rick Warren, when I was a Christian I used to preach that being a member of the "Army of God" or the "body of Christ" is more than a weekend sport. Jesus was the Lord, the King, the Coach, the Director not just of a movie or a team, but of your entire life. Christ was the Master, and we were the slaves. Look at the opening verses of these New Testament books:

> *"Paul, a slave of Jesus Christ, called to be an apostle, separated unto the gospel of God." (Romans 1:1)*

> *"Paul, a slave of God, and an apostle of Jesus Christ." (Titus 1:1)*

> *"James, a slave of God and of the Lord Jesus Christ." (James 1:1)*

> *"Jude, the slave of Jesus Christ." (Jude 1:1)*

> *"Simon Peter, a slave and apostle of Jesus Christ." (II Peter 1:1)*

If you look up these verses in most English-language bibles, you may see "servant" or "bondservant" instead of "slave." These euphemisms for the unambiguous Greek word *doulos*, which simply means "slave," have been in use since the bible was first translated into English, at a time when British society had many "servants" but few "slaves." In the Roman Empire, on the other hand, virtually all servants were slaves, though not all slaves were servants. Modern historians estimate that over 25 percent of the population of Rome, 30 to 40 percent of Italians, more than 50 percent of Gauls, and 75 to 90 percent of residents in some other parts of the empire were slaves, so the word *doulos* held no ambiguity for the people of Jesus' time.

The submission to someone who owns and controls your life is subjugation. Many modern translators, living in an enlightened world shaped by abolitionists, find it hard to imagine that their "Good Book" would actually endorse what we now know is abhorrent, so they substitute "servant" for "slave" to make the bible more palatable, if not more honest.

The early Christians were proud to be slaves! "If I was trying to please men," Paul wrote, "I would not be a slave of Christ." (Galatians 1:10) And it's not just the apostles. All Christians are required to "bring every thought into captivity unto the obedience of Christ." (II Corinthians 10:5) I don't know about you, but to me "captivity" does not sound like freedom—that verse sounds like a celebration of brainwashing and mind control. "If any man will come after me," Jesus said, "let him deny himself, take up his cross and follow me." That's slave talk.

In a 2007 sermon called "Slaves for Christ," evangelical preacher John MacArthur said:

> We are, as believers, slaves of Christ . . . You do have a personal relationship to Jesus Christ: you are His slave . . . When you give somebody the gospel, you are saying to them, "I would like to invite you to become a slave of Jesus Christ, to give up your independence, give up your freedom, submit yourself to an alien will, abandon all your rights, be owned by, controlled by the Lord." . . . We are slaves, happily so, gladly so.

According to Paul, we were sold at a slave auction: "For you were bought at a price; therefore glorify God in your body and in your spirit, which are God's." (I Corinthians 6:20) Temporary voluntary service to others is meritorious and can even provide some purpose in life if it is part of a plan of your choosing, but to be a slave and brag about it is sad. Worse, to want someone to be your slave is despicable.

If It's Friday, This Must Be Servitude

To comprehend the implications of slavery and servitude in Britain soon after the bible was translated into English and made widely available to lay readers, take another look at one of the first novels published in the English language, Daniel Defoe's immensely popular *Robinson Crusoe* (completed in 1720, about a century after the King James Bible, in which the word "servant" was substituted for "slave," became England's official bible). Defoe had plenty to say about slavery and Christianity in the British colonial era.

As a child, I was fascinated with the adventures of Robinson Crusoe, an English merchant who managed to survive after being shipwrecked on a deserted island, utilizing the available resources and his own ingenuity. My eyes widened as I imagined that lone bare footprint in the sand. It was high adventure, featuring two men from different cultures who become "buddies" and overcome difficulties together.

I recently decided to re-read Defoe's novel—the entire unabridged "adult" version—and discovered that it wasn't like that at all. This time I was shocked by what jumped out at me. In my youth, I hadn't realized that Crusoe was a slave trader himself, and apparently a missionary to the heathen as well.

Early in the novel, Crusoe is captured by Moorish pirates, who enslave him for two years. He finally escapes with the help of another slave, an Arab teenager named Xury. The two are rescued by a Portuguese ship bound for Brazil. There Crusoe buys a tract of land to turn into a plantation. How does he, a recently freed slave, get the money to pay for his land? Well, by selling Xury to the Portuguese captain as a slave! The irony is apparently lost on Crusoe, who sees no contradiction between the exploitation of a brown-skinned heathen Muslim and the natural rights of a white-skinned Christian Englishman created by God "in His own image," as Genesis 1:27 says, even though they served together as slaves on the same boat.

Crusoe does not simply accept slavery—he has a thirst for it. He later sets sail back across the Atlantic to bring slaves from Africa to work on his plantation, but a storm wrecks the ship on an island off the South American coast, and all the crew and passengers except him drown.

Over years of solitude, Crusoe learns that warlike Indians sometimes land on "his" island to hold cannibalistic rituals on the beach, during which they sacrifice other indigenous people they have captured. Hellbent on his original purpose of getting a slave of his own, Crusoe plots to "save" one of the victims. Watching carefully from a distance, he sees one of the prisoners bolt and run past him, then steps in and kills the two pursuers. The escapee, in gratitude and fear, kneels down to swear allegiance to his savior.

> And then he kneeled down again, kissed the ground, and
> laid his head upon the ground, and taking me by the foot,
> set my foot upon his head: this, it seems was in token of
> swearing to be my slave for ever . . . I made him know
> that his name should be Friday, which was the day I saved
> his life . . . I likewise taught him to say Master, and then
> let him know that was to be my name.

After 28 years, Crusoe is rescued, and Friday goes with him to travel the world as his servant (though there is no indication that he gets paid for his services). Crusoe discovers that the Portuguese sea captain from his youth has banked the profits from the Brazilian plantation and made him (though perhaps not Friday) a rich man. Returning from Portugal to England, the pair are attacked by wolves in the snow. Crusoe escapes, but Friday is devoured, having laid down his life for his master one last time.

Throughout their lives together, the Indian and the white man apparently never call each other by their real names, nor does either of them find anything unnatural about Friday's sacrificing his entire life by submitting to his "savior" as a slave. The implication is that slaves are voluntary participants in their own bondage. One would think that Crusoe, having saved a person's life, would be happy to know that he was free to resume his own life, perhaps to be reunited with his own people. Why should Friday throw away his future, forsaking his family and his own dreams, to spend all his time in the service of a hermit? To both men, "salvation"—specifically saving Friday's life—meant something far different than it would to us today. The whole scheme served to glorify Crusoe, not to truly save Friday. Crusoe's arrogance and greed are satisfied at the expense of denigrating Friday.

It may throw some light on Robinson Crusoe's world view to notice that one of the first things he does with his new slave is to convert him to Christianity. The story of "Master and Friday" comes across as a not-so-benign metaphor for "God and his *doulos*." Crusoe is deeply religious and thinks civilization requires adherence to the teachings of Jesus. Some scholars speculate that Defoe's choice of the name "Crusoe" was inspired by the word "cross," from the same Latin root word as "crusade" and "crucifixion." Historically, look what has happened when the purpose-driven Christians, bringing "glory to God," have come into contact with non-Christians, especially with "savages" and "infidels." Crusades, invasions, colonizations, exploitations, holy wars, and forced conversions—it happened in Africa and Hawaii, and to my family's native American ancestors, and everywhere else the "good news of the Gospel" was spread.

Of course, Robinson Crusoe's racial and religious attitudes likely were not shared by author Defoe, whose principal occupation was that of satirist and pamphleteer. *Robinson Crusoe* may have been a veiled satire. Defoe wrote and published more than 800 tracts, many of them veiled but no less scathing attacks on the government and the church. He had plenty of time to contemplate matters of freedom and isolation while serving several prison terms for his seditious pamphlets, as well as for nonpayment of debts. He also lived for years as a "Sunday gentleman"—a fugitive who only appeared in public on Sundays, when the law would not allow arrest warrants to be served. Whether he actually went to church is less clear, though.

When it came to religion, Defoe professed to be a Dissenter, part of a sect that opposed the established church institutions of the time. Some Rational Dissenter groups of Defoe's era evolved into the tolerant Quakers and liberal Unitarians of today.

Whether Defoe intended his novel as satirical or serious, the attitudes embodied by Robinson Crusoe present a disturbing view of the relationship between servitude and Christianity that persists to this day.

The Lord Taketh Away

Before we leave the colonial Caribbean, we might wonder what became of Friday's family. Near the end of the novel, Friday's father shows up, having paddled a canoe from his home on a larger island nearby that was occupied by Spaniards. Some scholars contend that the fictional island on which Crusoe and Friday were stranded was inspired by the real island of Tobago, near the larger island of Trinidad.

Author V. S. Naipaul was born in the town of Chaguanas, Trinidad. In his acceptance speech for the 2001 Nobel Prize in Literature, Naipaul said:

> One day in the British Museum I read a letter from the King of Spain to the governor of Trinidad. It was dated October 12, 1625. "I asked you," the king wrote, "to give me some information about a certain nation of Indians called Chaguanes, who you say number above one thousand, and are of such bad disposition that it was they who led the English when they captured the town. Their crime hasn't been punished because forces were not available for this purpose and because the Indians acknowledge no master save their own will. You have decided to give them a punishment. Follow the rules I have given you; and let me know how you get on."

This is a chilling letter. We don't know exactly how the Catholic Spanish governor managed to "get on" with the re-calcitrant indigenous people, but we do know that they were wiped off the planet. Today, Chaguanas is the largest and fastest-growing town on Trinidad. But something is missing. There is no trace of the Chaguanes people or their culture anywhere in Trinidad, an island named for the trinitarian deity of the Christian invaders. Those free local people, descendants of the early settlers of the island, were apparently exterminated in a holy genocide, all because of their "bad disposition" in resisting foreign invasion and Catholic conversion. They were punished for the crime of acknowledging "no master save their own will," for refusing to bow to the One True God. Because those natural human beings had their own purpose and did not submit to the "purpose of life" of bringing biblically mandated "glory" to the Lord of those violent dictators, they could not be tolerated. Since they were alive, and not biblically "dead unto themselves," they had to be made literally dead.

I don't believe in God, but even if he did exist, and even if he did save my life, I'd find it hard to imagine that he would be the kind of creature who would demand that I submit to his will. Even if such primitive attitudes prevailed in the 17th and 18th centuries, it seems bizarre that they should survive today, with our hard-fought gains in civil liberties, our advances in education and instant worldwide communication. Yet believers still flock to church to sing "To God be the glory" and "Crown Him with many crowns" in the belief that their purpose comes from bowing to a king or governor. If there were such a God, demanding that servants kneel before him, glorifying his name, why should we respect him? Even if we were oppressed people who wanted to avoid the wrath of a ruler who had the power to punish and kill, we might pretend to go along by kissing the feet of our oppressor, but why should anyone think such a master deserves to be admired?

Suppose I decided to breed children as slaves. What would you think of me? Yes, there would be purpose involved, but it would be my own selfish purpose of needing to be doted and waited upon. Those children would exist for my satisfaction, with no free purpose of their own. That would make me an egotistical monster.

One of the most circular yet revealing verses in the bible is Revelation 4:11: "Thou art worthy, O Lord, to receive glory and honor and power: for thou hast created all things, and for thy pleasure they are and were created." In other words, the reason we should admire God is because he created us to admire him. Isn't "I brought you into this world to praise me, which is why you should praise me" the kind of power every megalomaniacal dictator dreams of?

Praise and worship are two different things. There is nothing wrong with praise, if the object of our admiration has earned it. But worship signals inferiority and subjugation. Worship is a humbling denial of your own value in order to inflate someone else's worth. Look at the postures of prayer. They are identical to the postures of captivity and slavery: head bowed, knees bent, hands shackled at the wrists, body prostrated, eyes closed, voice lowered—all to be submissive and nonthreatening before a great master who demands to be feared, served, and adored. The forced or mandated subjugation of "inferior people" by a "superior person" is evidence that the ruler is actually insecure, scared of any possible challenge to his authority, jealous of any praise not directed at *his* person, craving all the attention, fearful of freedom, nervous about rebellion—otherwise, why coerce or demand submission? If there truly were an all-powerful and unchallengeable god, why would he need or want to be worshipped? What is he afraid of? In any master/slave or dictator/servant arrangement, I wonder who is more fearful—the sovereign or the subjects? All human captors understand that at heart every human being desires freedom—they know that *they* would hate to be enslaved—so they must do everything possible to prevent the underlings from acting the same way they would if the tables were turned. Since God, if he exists, needs to be worshipped, then he is not God. Glory undermines power. Glory is insecurity masquerading as unearned praise.

Many of the Guineamen slave ships crossing the Atlantic in slave-trading days had netting around the outside to catch those captured Africans who tried to jump into the water. Technically they were not slaves yet, and many preferred to knowingly leap to the sharks instead of submitting to the horror of becoming someone else's property. Slavery is not natural—at least not to the slave—and anyone who practices or promotes it is immoral.

Asking, "If there is no God, what is the purpose of life?" is like asking, "If there is no master, whose slave will I be?" If your purpose of life is to submit as a slave, then your meaning comes from flattering the ego of a person whom you should detest. Wouldn't it be *more* meaningful if there were no purpose, no slavery at all? Why do we bend our brains in the direction of servitude? Why do we think life has to "have a purpose"? Who made the rule that existence is meaningless if it is free?

Owning Your Purpose

It *is* about you. Contrary to Rick Warren's demeaning advice, your purpose is about you—and no one else.

Not everything is about you. Morality is how you treat your neighbor. Truth is how well your statements match reality. Behavior and opinions can be right or wrong. But purpose is entirely different. Your purpose is how you choose to live your own life. No priest, pastor, parent, rabbi, imam, mullah, witch doctor, governor, monarch, god, or holy book—or this book—can dictate your purpose in life. You decide. Otherwise, you are a slave.

In my own experience, the greatest benefit of being an atheist is the freedom to think my own thoughts, to live my own life. Every healthy organism wants the liberty to pursue its own goals. An animal may sometimes feel safer inside a cage, but does it want to be there? How many zebras, dolphins, and parrots willingly stay in captivity? Open the door and watch what happens. The nature of life is freedom, with all its rewards and risks, and if you don't have that freedom, you don't have a life. One may sometimes sacrifice, limit, and deny oneself to help or cooperate with others, but that is a willing choice, a part of one's own freely chosen purpose in life.

Purpose is striving for a goal, intentionally aiming at a target. Purpose is life. There is no striving without a reason, and the reason always has something to do with surviving and enjoying your life. If you are not enjoying life—or at least striving to flourish and enjoy life—you are not living your life. Enjoyment is not a thing that exists for its own sake. When you are walking or running somewhere, for example, your purpose is to get from point A to point B for a reason. (Point B might be a moving target, or at an unknown location, in which case you are searching.) The reason might be the need for food to satisfy hunger or water to slake thirst—in other words, personal survival—and look how much enjoyment we get from it. Your purpose might be shelter or safety, protection from the threat of the elements and predators. Look how much we enjoy a warm fire during a blizzard or an air-conditioned room during a heat wave. It might be a mate, so your genes and our species will survive (and I don't need to say how much we enjoy *that!*). It might be physical exercise to keep yourself healthy so you can meet challenges and live longer—and look at the "high" some people get from the sheer act of exercising. These goals and others, when obtained by some kind of striving, are pleasurable because they relate to survival. Less tangible goals such as beauty, love, friendship, learning, adventure, and entertainment, all with their built-in risks as well as rewards—are enjoyable because they contribute to well-being and so enhance survival. Even indirect goals, such as helping others to survive, are pleasurable. That is your life. That is what purpose means.

All living things have purpose. You don't even need a brain. When a plant turns toward the sun, it is striving to reach a goal. When tree roots grope toward the river, they are aiming for a target. Life is purpose, and purpose is life. Asking "What is the purpose of life?" is asking "What is the life of life?" And that is completely backward. Such a question is based on the assumption that life is not life. If you don't have the freedom to choose to strive for your own goals, then you are dead. If you think your purpose must come from outside yourself, you are a slave to another mind.

That is exactly what most religions teach. Christianity, for example, cheats it followers with the sleight-of-hand of trading purpose for purpose, euthanizing the individual by cutting out the heart of his or her purpose and moving it outside of the individual.

There Is No Purpose of Life

Life is its own reward. To live freely is to escape from the tyranny of a sovereign. It is to start a proud revolutionary war defying the king with a Declaration of Independence, protesting that when people are subjugated "under absolute Despotism, it is their right, it is their duty, to throw off such Government." Is there anything more noble or exciting than a slave revolt? Real living comes from getting rid of an externally imposed purpose. There is no purpose of life—nor should we want there to be. Unshackled from the chains of a master, we are truly free to live.

When a new baby comes into the world, we don't say, "How sweet! Another worker for the cause. Another laborer for the plantation. Another cog in the machine. Another soldier marching off to war. Another voice to sing praises to our Master!" What an insult to a new life! If a baby is born with preordained orders, then its life is cheapened. A "purpose of life" is a kind of child abuse. A purpose-driven life is one that has been hijacked and diminished. It loses autonomy. If life has a purpose, we are tools or slaves, pack animals following the leader, carrying someone else's load. We relinquish the liberty to chart our own course, wend our own way, make our own discoveries, create our own purpose.

Although there is no purpose of life—and it is wonderful that there isn't—you can still have a purpose-filled life. To say there is no purpose *of* life does not mean there is no purpose *in* life.* Your life has purpose not because it is bestowed by an entity outside yourself but because you bestow it by your own mind. One is bondage, the other is liberty.

---

*I first heard it phrased like this by philosopher Kai Nielsen: "If there is no God, it is indeed true that we are not blessed with the questionable blessing of being made for a purpose; furthermore, if there is neither God nor Logos, there is no purpose to life, no plan for the universe or providential ordering of things in accordance with which we must live our lives. Yet, from the fact, if it is a fact, that there is no purpose to life or no purposes for which we are made, it does not at all follow that there are no purposes in life that are worth achieving, doing, or having, so that life in reality must be just one damn thing after another that finally, senselessly terminates in death. . . . In a Godless world, in which death is inevitable, our lives are not robbed of meaning." *Ethics Without God*, by Kai Nielsen (Prometheus Books, 1990).

Purpose is not something you search for. It is not something you find. It is not endowed by a creator or handed to you by your parents or government. It is something *you* choose to create. If you permit the mind of a mythical God, who does not even exist, to bestow purpose, why deny it of your own mind, which *does* exist?

Purpose comes from solving problems. As long as there are challenges, there is purpose in life. All intentional activity is solving some kind of problem—the huge problems of survival or the simple problems of how to get things done. A bigger problem simply brings a bigger purpose. It is fruitless to launch a quest for "the purpose of life." There is no such thing. You don't look for an intention before you know what you want or need to do. It is only after you identify a lack, or desire, or value, or goal, that you "head for it." The "heading for" is the intention in action. It is the very struggle to solve problems that makes life what it is.

Life is not driven by purpose; purpose is driven by life.

Hoping for a heaven without struggle is longing for a life without purpose. There is no purpose in glory. Glorifying God is not a problem to solve. Why does he need to be glorified? If he does, his life lacks something, and that would be an embarrassing admission for a perfect being to make. Striving to fulfill that need in *his* empty life might give *him* purpose, but not us. To glorify is to fatten up someone's ego. Why do that? Are you afraid you will be killed, hurt or denied a blessing if you don't help the "Lord and Master" feel great? If so, you are being manipulated to meet someone else's need. Glorifying is placating, pleading, begging, hoping to be recognized as a useful servant, desiring to be in the good graces of a person who can reward or hurt you. "Fear not them which kill the body, but are not able to kill the soul," Jesus reportedly said, "but rather fear him which is able to destroy both soul and body in hell." (Matthew 12:10) Purpose can indeed be motivated by fear, and tackling the frightening problems that threaten survival is certainly useful. But the ideal way—the moral way—to handle a tyrant is to overthrow him, not enable him.

If you are still religious and are struggling with "what it all means," here is something purposeful to do: get rid of the problem. Start a slave rebellion. Honor the American rebels and other revolutionaries around the world, and snub the sovereign. Depose the dictator and live your own life.

A Super Natural Life

I used to think I had a life of purpose when I was spreading the Gospel and "glorifying God," but now I see that that was a cheap substitute for life. I didn't reject Christianity because I failed to understand it—if I was not a true Christian, then nobody is. I rejected it because it is insulting to life and freedom, not to mention that it is untrue. Since the real world is the only world that matters, preaching a nonexistent fantasy world is a huge waste of time. I believed it all, utterly and completely, to the point where I dedicated my life to the service of Jesus, but I now see how thin and artificial the fantasy was. Pretending that doing nothing is actually meaningful, I gained immense unearned respect from pew-sitters who desperately wanted someone else to tell them how to live, how to think, how to "find purpose" in their lives. There would be no shepherds without sheep. Like Rick Warren, I found a calling—a so-called purpose-driven life—because so many other people believe purpose must come from outside themselves.

My life of ministry was the beneficiary of this upside-down religious mindset.

In *Reason Driven Life,* Robert Price, another fundamentalist preacher who eventually saw the light, compares humanism with superstition and aptly describes the mentality of sheep seeking a shepherd:

> *On the other hand, there is Rick Warren's type of Christian morality: the morality of the slaves, of the huddling herd. This is the code of the cringing, the cowardly, those who herd together for mutual sympathy and comfort, who dare not rise above the common level of mediocrity lest they be struck down. They want to play it safe. They worship the tyrant that enslaves them, being infected with what we now call the Stockholm syndrome, the pathetic transfer of affections from one's captors and tormentors. The slave professes himself, and truly believes himself, happy to suffer punishment from his masters, since he must have deserved it, and it must be for his own good. He does not presume to think any thought not preapproved by the guardians of orthodoxy, and he whispers warnings to questioning souls not to heed the seductions of Satan. He exalts humility as it is usually defined, a self-abnegating dismissal of one's own value, for this is a way of internalizing the contempt of one's master and thus avoiding the risk of being struck down by him.*

It wasn't until I got out of the master/slave business that I learned what true purpose is. It comes from solving real problems, not phony ones such as "how can I be saved?"

We are biological organisms in a natural environment. That is all, and that is enough. My wife, Annie Laurie, likes to say, "The natural world is super enough for me." It is more than enough. We get to *live*. That is better than having a purpose. How sad to think that there has to be a meaning to it all. Life is life. The demand for a purpose of life is a cry of discontent. To reach outside your life for meaning is to abandon the value of what is inside your life. It is to diminish and deny the value of life itself. It is to be embarrassed at who you really are. Transcendence is the ultimate put-down of humanity.

Life doesn't need purpose: Purpose needs life. We know, learn or decide what we value and then work to protect and promote what we value. We solve problems. The environment can be harsh, so we build housing and make clothing. Illness can kill or maim, so we experiment with medicine or diet or prevention or life-style changes to combat it. Food and goods need to be distributed, so we build railroads and software to run them. A percentage of people will be criminal or mentally unhealthy, threatening the rest of us, so we come up with a system of justice, prisons, and mental hospitals, as well as measures to treat and try to cure those who are ill. These are all material, biological endeavors.

Do you want a purpose-filled life? Find a problem to solve. Do what your ancestors did: If they had not struggled, you would not be here. Purpose is mainly about finding solutions. If you are trying to eliminate a threat to survival or to enhance the opportunities for a quality life, you have purpose. Find something you hate and work against it. Find something you love and work for it. Hunger, natural disasters, inequality, oppression, unfairness, predation, disease, invasions, aggression, racism, sexism, cruelty to animals, pollution, endangered species, political corruption, corporate greed, unsafe working conditions, exploitation—these are all worth fighting. The toil to gain scientific and historical knowledge; or the exercise of creating beauty, art, music, literature, theater, and architecture; or the efforts put into sports, entertainment, cooking, and gardening—these are all worthwhile, useful, and purpose-filled activities, and you can probably think of more. Problems improve and enrich life. Purpose does not come from puffing up the glory of an imaginary praise-hungry slavemaster in a magical world, but from solving problems to make a better place of this, the only world we have.

Robert G. Ingersoll, the great 19th-century agnostic orator, said it well:

> *The hands that help are better far*
> *Than lips that pray.*
> *Love is the ever gleaming star*
> *That leads the way,*
> *That shines, not on vague worlds of bliss,*
> *But on a paradise in this.*

PART 2

Profiles in
Nonbelief

HOPE IS INDEED VALUABLE, but it is only meaningful if it is realistic. I might hope to be seven feet tall or possess magical powers, but that is not going to happen. Rather than investing time and energy hoping for eternal life in a fanciful supernatural world, nonbelievers focus on goals that have a reasonable chance of being reached. In fact, we atheists and agnostics feel that it is the believers who have been effectively neutered and made hopeless, since they are placing their bet on winning the cosmic lottery in an attempt to be "saved" from their aimless lives—or from the lives that their pastor tells them are aimless. A normal lottery ticket is statistical theft, but a lottery ticket with a zero chance of paying off is pure robbery. If they realized that their lives already have purpose, believers would not need to purchase it from God, the bible, or shell-game con artists like Rick Warren.

Most Christians are indeed good people who live lives of immense purpose, but this is not because it was handed to them by their faith or their god. It is because Christians live in the same natural world as everyone else. We all raise families and work meaningful jobs. We all create works of art and volunteer to help others. Believers and nonbelievers are no different in that regard. For preachers to claim that those of us who do not believe in God or live to bring "glory" to a deity are "purposeless" is similar to the discriminatory smearing of gays as "dissolute," or Jews as "uncouth," or blacks as "shiftless." Atheophobia should be just as unacceptable as homophobia, anti-Semitism, or racism.

The best way to reduce prejudice is to meet some of the people whom you thought were untouchable. This is what has happened in the gay movement, and although homosexuals still have a long way to go, they have made impressive strides in recent decades by coming out of the closet. Atheists are now doing the same thing, earning the nickname "New Atheists" as a result. There is nothing new about atheism, but what is indeed novel is the fact that many more of us are coming out into the open. I invite Rick Warren to read the following pages spotlighting the lives of hundreds of out-of-the-closet atheists and agnostics (and a few skeptical deists) and then dare him to continue preaching the discriminatory falsehood that nonbelievers have no purpose.

None of the people profiled in this book had or have "purpose-driven lives." They have purpose-*filled* lives—purpose that is driven by life itself, not the other way around. If you want a purpose-filled life, like these people, then get to work. There are many challenges in the real world that directly confront you. Focus on one of those real problems, not on an imaginary magical savior whom you hope will make it easy for you. Believing in a god is a cheap shot, a lazy grab to win the lottery of life, a way to cheat on the test by letting someone else do the work. When it comes to purpose, faith is irrelevant, impractical, and distracting. The next time someone tells you there is no purpose without God, tell them about the millions of us who live happy, productive, meaningful, moral, and purpose-filled lives without God.

Actors

What do Harry Potter, Elmer Gantry, Indiana Jones, Prissy, Don Vito Corleone, and Androgynous Pat have in common? Besides being fictional characters, they were all played by actors who do not believe in God. Many atheists, agnostics, and religious skeptics have created purpose by creating characters whose stories enrich our lives.

Woody Allen

(1935–) | actor, director

"Not only is there no God, but try getting a plumber on weekends," Allen quipped. He also said, "I'm agnostic, but I have one foot in atheism." His autobiographical *Stardust Memories* contains an Allen character who quips, "To you, I'm an atheist. To God, I'm the loyal opposition." In his book, *Without Feathers*, Allen wrote: "How can I believe in God when just last week I got my tongue caught in the roller of an electric typewriter?"

Janeane Garofalo

(1964–) | actress, stand-up comedian

Garofalo has been an outspoken critic of religion. Recording an ad for the Freedom From Religion Foundation, she ended with the phrase: "Proud to be an atheist! Janeane Garofalo." Also a noted peace activist, Garofalo has said, "[God] just seems very man-made to me . . . It's human nature to need a religious crutch, and I don't begrudge anyone that. I just don't need one." In her book, *Feel This Book,* she wrote:

Organized religions and their dogmas only serve to indoc-
trinate the participants into sheeplike common behaviors.
This type of blind assimilation promotes the popularity of
top-forty count-down radio stations and movie sequels.
Skepticism towards groups, holy or otherwise, is enriching
and makes you a far more entertaining person.

Ricky Gervais

(1961–) | comedian, actor, director, producer, screenwriter
Gervais's Web site has an article titled "My Argument
With God: How I went from Jesus-loving Christian to
fun-loving infidel . . . in one afternoon," in which he
tells about the day when he was about eight years old,
drawing Jesus on the cross. His brother asked him why
he believed in God and his mother was mortified at the
question. Gervais thought, "Why was that a bad thing to
ask? If there was a god and my faith was strong, it didn't
matter what people thought. Oh . . . hang on. There is no
God. He knows it, and she knows it deep down. It was
as simple as that. I started thinking about it and asking
more questions, and within an hour I was an atheist."
Realizing that his normally honest mother had not told
the truth, he forgave her: "It's always better to tell the
truth. The truth doesn't hurt, and saying that, my mother
only ever lied to me about one thing. She said there was
a God. But that's because when you're a working-class
mum, Jesus is like an unpaid baby-sitter." He told James
Lipton, "If there is a God, why did he make me an atheist? That was his first mistake."

Terry Jones

(1942–) | *comedian, writer, director*

This co-creator of the classic British comedy TV show
Monty Python's Flying Circus is completely irreverent. "I
have no sympathy whatever [for Christianity]," he said
during an interview. "Any religion that makes a form
of torture into an icon that they worship seems to me
a pretty sick kind of religion, quite honestly." Talking
about religious reactions to the movie *The Life of Brian*,
Jones said: "Maybe it is being offensive to them, because
it is making fun of people who don't think for themselves, and that's exactly what the whole film's about.
So I think it's quite right for people who don't think for
themselves to get upset about it."

Burt Lancaster

(1913–1994) | *actor*

A self-described atheist, Lancaster turned down the role
of Ben-Hur, but accepted the part of corrupt evangelist
Elmer Gantry, for which he won a Best Actor Oscar,
because he wanted to make an anti–Billy Graham statement. In an ad Lancaster recorded for the ACLU, confess-
ing that he was a "card-carrying member," he said: "No
one agrees with every single thing they've done. But no
one can disagree with the guiding principle—with liberty
and justice for all."

Butterfly McQueen

(1911–1995) | *actress*

Best known for her role as Prissy in *Gone with the Wind*,
McQueen was a life member of the Freedom From Reli-

gion Foundation. She was very smart and resented being typecast in the role of servant. "As my ancestors are free from slavery, I am free from the slavery of religion," she told the *Atlanta Journal & Constitution* in 1989, on the 50th anniversary of *Gone with the Wind*.

Paul Newman
(1925–2008) | *actor*
Although Paul Newman had no religion as an adult, his father was a nonpracticing Jew, and his mother was a tolerant Christian Scientist who didn't mind that her sons were not following her faith. Writes biographer Shawn Levy:

> *The prevailing religion of the [Newman] household seemed, in fact, to be Americanism. The Newman boys received no formal religious instruction after grade school, and later on Paul would come more or less to see himself as an areligious Jew. He was so out of touch with the faith, though, that he was once caught by a journalist declaring frustration at not being able to reach anybody in the movie business on the phone—only to learn to his surprise that it was, in fact, Yom Kippur.*

Joaquin Phoenix
(1974–) | *actor*
Phoenix was born to Children of God missionaries in Puerto Rico but became disillusioned with the cult and left when he was a small child. Outspoken about his atheism, Joaquin told the *Sunday Times*, "I'm not into organized religion . . . For me, I believe in a God of whatever my own thing is." To *Nylon Guys* magazine, he said: "I don't believe in god. I don't believe in an afterlife. I don't

believe in soul. I don't believe in anything. I think it's totally right for people to have their own beliefs if it makes them happy, but to me it's a pretty preposterous idea."

More actors' quotes about religion

"Prayers never bring anything. . . . They may bring solace to the sap, the bigot, the ignorant, the aboriginal, and the lazy—but to the enlightened it is the same as asking Santa Claus to bring you something for Xmas."
   —W. C. Fields

"In Philadelphia, I inadvertently came upon an edition of Robert Ingersoll's Essays and Lectures. This was an exciting discovery; his atheism confirmed my own belief that the horrific cruelty of the Old Testament was degrading to the human spirit."
   —Charlie Chaplin

"Although we weren't brought up to be any particular religion, we were taught to say our prayers. I remember one that ended, 'Thy glorious kingdom, which is for ever and ever. Amen.' These words made me scream, 'I don't want to be anywhere for ever and ever. It's too much.'"
   —Hermione Gingold

"I lost my faith during the war and can't believe they are all up there, flying around or sitting at tables, all those I've lost."
   —Marlene Dietrich

"To be perfectly frank, I really do not [believe in God]."
   —Bruce Lee

"Obviously, all religions get corrupted by man. The initial ideas are interesting, but once they get organized, they seem to become about politics and other things and they get misinterpreted. . . . Have faith, but do the work. Live your life right. Don't expect things to happen. That's why I'm put off by magical realism."
     —**Matt Dillon**

"[Buddhism] deals with the fact, in essence, you know, come right out and say it, that there is no God, that the individual is God."
     —**Patrick Duffy**

"There had never been any renunciation of religion on my part, but like so many people, it was a gradual fading away."
     —**Henry Fonda**

"I'm an atheist, and that's it. I believe there's nothing we can know except that we should be kind to each other and do what we can for each other."
     —**Katharine Hepburn**

"My parents did not practice any organized religion, although my father was raised Roman Catholic and my mother was Jewish. But there was always an ethical context to our lives, a very strong notion of individual moral responsibility."
     —**Harrison Ford**

"I follow no doctrine. I don't belong to a church or a temple or a synagogue or an ashram.
     —**Meryl Streep**

Doubt is our friend. And once you tip the scales in one direction or another it's very, very dangerous."
  —**Meryl Streep**

"More wars have been fought in the name of religion than any other cause. More people have been persecuted, reputations ruined, and fortunes plundered and murders committed in the name of religion than any other enterprise. And more everyday bigotry and prejudice is founded on what religion a person follows than any other factor . . . Forget believing in God. How about thinking for yourself on any subject! Bottom line—I don't care what you believe, or what church you attend, or how religion-oriented your private life is. Keep it out of my government. Keep it out of my laws. Keep it out of my bedroom. And keep it out of the war rooms at the Pentagon!"
  —**Harvey Fierstein**

"Organized religions in general, in my opinion, are dying forms. They were all very important when we didn't know why the sun moved, why weather changed, why hurricanes occurred, or volcanoes happened. Modern religion is the end trail of modern mythology. But there are people who interpret the Bible literally. Literally! I choose not to believe that's the way. And that's what makes America cool, you know?"
  —**Bruce Willis**

"I'm an atheist; I suppose you can call me a sort of libertarian anarchist. I regard religion with fear and suspicion. It's not enough to say that I don't believe in God. I

actually regard the system as distressing: I am offended by some of the things said in the Bible and the Koran, and I refute them."
  —**Emma Thompson**

"I don't believe in heaven and hell. I don't know if I believe in God. All I know is that as an individual, I won't allow this life—the only thing I know to exist—to be wasted."
  —**George Clooney**

"Believing in Santa Claus is sort of like believing in God. If you want to do it, that's fine. Just don't ask too many questions.
  —**Julia Sweeney**

It took me years, but letting go of religion has been the most profound wake-up of my life. I feel I now look at the world not as a child, but as an adult. I see what's bad, and it's really bad. But I also see what is beautiful, what is wonderful. And I feel so deeply appreciative that I am alive. How dare the religious use the term 'born again.' That truly describes freethinkers who've thrown off the shackles of religion so much better!"
  —**Julia Sweeney**

"I do realize that the word 'believe' is part of the word 'faith.' And I don't believe in God. So I'm a non-believer in the non-visible. I'm a believer in us; in humans."
  —**Eddie Izzard**

"[T]here is no direct evidence, so how could you ask me to believe in God when there's absolutely no evidence that I can see? I do believe in the beauty and the awe-inspiring mystery of the science that's out there that we haven't discovered yet, that there are scientific explanations for phenomena that we call mystical because we don't know any better."

—Jodie Foster

"When I got untethered from the comfort of religion, it wasn't a loss of faith for me. It was a discovery of self. I had thought that I'm capable enough to handle any situation. There's peace in understanding that I have only one life, here and now, and I'm responsible."

—Brad Pitt

"I don't have a chance [on being elected Mayor of New Orleans]. I'm running on the gay marriage, no religion, legalization and taxation of marijuana platform."

—Brad Pitt

"I'm an atheist. My mother is very religious, a churchgoer. . . . There was no defining moment in which I decided there was no god for me. It was more of a growing process. I do feel that whatever religious beliefs I had as a child were foisted upon me. It's like when you ask where Grandma went when she died, and you'd be told that she went to heaven. I wouldn't necessarily view that as a bad thing, but it was stuff like that which I think hindered my intellectual development. Now that I've grown, I prefer a different interpretation."

—Christopher Eccleston

"I wondered a little why God was such a useless thing. It seemed a waste of time to have him. After that he became less and less, until he was . . . nothingness."

—Frances Farmer

"I wish I believed I'd see my parents again, see my wife again. But I know it's not going to happen."
—**Tony Randall**

"I will not swear on God. I will not swear on God, because I don't believe in the conceptual sense and in this nonsense. What I will swear on is my children and my grandchildren."
—**Marlon Brando**
testifying at the trial of his son Christian

"That's all religion is—some principle you believe in . . . man has accomplished far more miracles than the God he invented. What a tragedy it is to invent a God and then suffer to keep him King."
—**Rod Steiger**

"There's an old saying that God exists in your search for him. I just want you to understand that I ain't looking."
—**Leslie Nielsen**

"I've been so relieved and so grateful to not have a god to believe in."
—**Cloris Leachman**

"I don't believe in God now. My ethics basically are to live in the now, and that requires tremendous discipline. It's as close to a religious sentiment that I have."
—**Jack Nicholson**

"Think about it: religion has actually convinced people—many of them adults—that there's an invisible man living in the sky who watches everything you do, every minute of every day. And who has a special list of ten things he does not want you to do. And if you do *any* of these ten things, he has a special place, full of fire and smoke and burning and torture and anguish, where he will send you to remain and suffer and burn and choke and scream and cry, forever and ever, 'til the end of time! But He loves you. He loves you, and He needs money! He always needs money! He's all-powerful, all-perfect, all-knowing, and all-wise, somehow . . . he just can't handle money. Religion takes in billions of dollars, pays no taxes, and somehow always need a little more."

—George Carlin

"There doesn't need to be a God for me."

—Angelina Jolie

"I'm much more like the product of a doctor than I am a Jew."

—Natalie Portman

"I don't believe in [the afterlife]. I believe this is it, and I believe it's the best way to live."

—Natalie Portman

"I'm an atheist, but I'm relaxed about it. I don't preach my atheism, but I have a huge amount of respect for people like Richard Dawkins who do. Anything he does on television, I will watch. . . . There we go, Dan, that's half of America that's not going to see the next Harry Potter film on the back of that comment."

—Daniel Radcliffe

Artists

The creation of visual art is a high purpose. No act is more especially human than the communication of an idea, or a feeling—or simply beauty for the sake of beauty—through an artistic medium such as painting, drawing, or sculpting. They are more moving, meaningful, and relevant than any religious ministry.

Steve Benson

(1954–) | cartoonist

This Pulitzer Prize–winning cartoonist, who has been the editorial cartoonist at the *Arizona Republic* since 1980, is a former Mormon missionary, grandson of former Mormon president Ezra Taft Benson, Steve made a very public break with his church in 1993, citing "disagreement over its doctrines on race, women, intellectual freedom, and fanciful storytelling." Among the benefits of leaving religion, Benson lists: "another day off, a 10 percent raise, and getting to choose my own underwear." Benson and I co-produce the *Tunes 'n Toons* show, an irreverent look at religion in the news, combining cartoons, music and satire. "If, as the true believers claim, the word 'gospel' means good news," Benson said, "then the good news for me is that there is no gospel, other than what I can define for myself, by observation and conscience. As a freethinking human being, I have come not to favor or fear religion, but to face and fight it as an impediment to civilized advancement."

Bill Blass

(1922–2002) | *fashion designer*

Bill Blass was involved in community work throughout his life and was awarded several public service awards. He was a trustee of the New York Public Library. He told the SF Weekly: "I have a firm belief in such things as, you know, the water, the Earth, the trees and sky. And I'm wondering, it is increasingly difficult to find those elements in nature, because it's nature I believe in rather than some spiritual thing." Asked if he was a religious man, he replied, "No. And I do suppose that science has taken, to a large extent and for a number of people, has taken the place of religion. . . . That one can have more belief in scientific cures or scientific miracles than you do in God miracles. It's inevitable that we will eventually diffuse into nothingness."

Frida Kahlo

(1907–1954) | *painter*

Though raised by a Spanish Catholic mother and German Lutheran father, the trials of surviving polio and a devastating bus crash pushed the Mexican artist to reject conventional religion, a view reinforced by her friendship with Russian revolutionary Leon Trotsky. Kahlo often wove blasphemous themes and Catholic, Jewish, and pre-Columbian Indian symbolism into her surrealist paintings. Unhappy with the United States, she painted a montage that included a dollar sign wrapped across the cross on a church.

Henri Matisse

(1869–1954) | painter, sculptor, printmaker

"A staunch atheist," was how biographer Henry Spurling characterized the prolific French artist's religious attitude. "Ever since there have been men," Matisse said (paraphrasing Nietzsche), "man has given himself over to too little joy. That alone, my brothers, is our original sin. I should believe only in a God who understood how to dance."

Auguste Rodin

(1840–1917) | sculptor

Best known for his bronze sculptures *The Thinker* (a favorite among freethinkers) and *The Kiss*, Rodin briefly entered a sacred order after the death of his sister but soon realized he was not a man of faith. He was "independent of any religious doctrine," his biographer wrote.

Edward Sorel

(1929–) | illustrator

The New York illustrator, artist, and satirist is a member of the Freedom From Religion Foundation's Honorary Board. He is a regular contributor to *The Atlantic*, *The New Yorker,* and many other publications. In addition to more than 40 covers for *The New Yorker*, Sorel's art has appeared on the covers of *The Atlantic, Harpers, Fortune, Forbes, The Nation, Esquire, American Heritage*, and *The New York Times Magazine*. "I'm one of those who regard organized religion as a dangerous force. I try whenever possible to do anti-clerical cartoons," he told *The Atlantic*. Asked if he said he hated the Bush administration and Saddam Hussein, he replied: "All I said was that we have our religious fanatics fighting their religious fanatics, which leaves me without a side to root for." His 1992 drawing of "The Last Flossing" is pointedly irreverent.

Joseph Turner
(1775–1851) | painter
The English artist, who specialized in seascapes and romantic visions of nature, was not a religious person. Art critic John Ruskin often called him an "infidel." Biographers have written that he "did not profess to be a member of any visible church," and "had not a particle of religious belief, and rarely gave a thought to religion."

More artists' quotes about religion
"I believe in God, only I spell it Nature."
   —Frank Lloyd Wright

Authors

Many writers have been free from faith. The ability to think outside the religion box can offer a fresh perspective, challenging established notions.

Isaac Asimov
(1920–1992) | author, biochemistry professor
On coming to terms with his atheism, Asimov wrote:

> *I've been an atheist for years and years, but somehow I felt it was intellectually unrespectable to say one was an atheist, because it assumed knowledge that one didn't*

have. Somehow, it was better to say one was a humanist
or an agnostic. I finally decided that I'm a creature of emo-
tion as well as of reason. Emotionally, I am an atheist. I
don't have the evidence to prove that God doesn't exist, but
I so strongly suspect he doesn't that I don't want to waste
my time.

Asimov's 500-plus books span every category of the
Dewey Decimal System. "I don't believe in an afterlife, so
I don't have to spend my whole life fearing hell, or fear-
ing heaven even more. For whatever the tortures of hell,
I think the boredom of heaven would be even worse."
He wrote an entire book about the bible, *Asimov's Guide*
to the Bible, and he said, "Properly read, the Bible is the
most potent force for atheism ever conceived."

Pearl S. Buck

(1892–1973) | novelist, human rights activist
The daughter of Presbyterian missionaries, Buck lived
more than half her life in China. Her novel *The Good*
Earth won a Pulitzer Prize and was the best-selling book
in the United States for two years, and she subsequently
became the first woman to win a Nobel Prize for Literature. The novelist said, "I feel no need for any other faith
than my faith in human beings. Like Confucius of old, I
am so absorbed in the wonder of earth and the life upon
it that I cannot think of heaven and the angels." Besides
writing more than 70 books, Buck advocated for civil
rights and women's rights, was routinely published in the
NAACP's magazine, *Crisis*, and by the Urban League. She
was a 20-year trustee of Howard University. She founded
the first international interracial adoption agency, Wel-

come House, which placed more than 5,000 children in homes. In 1964, she started the Pearl S. Buck Foundation to help Amerasian children. "It may be that religion is dead," she wrote, "and if it is, we had better know it and set ourselves to try to discover other sources of moral strength before it is too late."

Samuel Clemens (Mark Twain)
(1835–1910) | journalist, novelist
The sardonic, irreverent Mark Twain (Samuel Clemens) wrote in *Puddinhead Wilson*: "Faith is believing what you know ain't so." His freethinking book, *Letters from the Earth*, was considered so blasphemous that it was not published until after his death. His 1905 "War Prayer" (not published until 1923) is a scathing indictment of war and religious hypocrisy. "I cannot see how a man of any large degree of humorous perception can ever be religious," Twain wrote in his journal, "except he purposely shut the eyes of his mind & keep them shut by force."

Edward Clodd
(1840–1930) | writer, anthropologist, folklorist
A philosophical ally of evolutionist Charles Darwin, Clodd wrote biographies of Darwin, Thomas Huxley, and Herbert Spencer, as well as *The Story of Creation: A Plain Account of Evolution*. He said, " . . . [T]he mysteries, on belief in which theology would hang the destinies of mankind, are cunningly devised fables whose origin and growth are traceable to the age of Ignorance, the mother of credulity."

Anthony Collins

(1676–1729) | *philosopher*
Called the "Goliath of freethinking" by Thomas Henry
Huxley and praised by Voltaire, Collins wrote many
books, including the influential *Discourse on Freethink-*
ing in 1713. He did not call himself an atheist, but was
a deist and materialist who opposed "priestcraft." His
writings helped to popularize the word "freethought,"
which he described as: "The Use of the Understanding,
in endeavouring to find out the Meaning of any Proposi-
tion whatsoever, in considering the nature and Evidence
for or against it, and in judging of it according to the
seeming Force or Weakness of the Evidence."

George Eliot

(1819–1880) | *novelist*
Raised a Christian, Mary Anne Evans, who used a male
pen name so her works would be taken seriously, rebelled
from the faith and was shunned by her family but remained a freethinker. Her poem, "O May I Join the Choir
Invisible" expressed her dismissal of the afterlife: "O may
I join the choir invisible/ Of those immortal dead who
live again/ In minds made better by their presence. . ."

Zona Gale

(1874–1938) | *author, playwright, women's rights activist*
This progressive feminist author, the first woman ever to
win the Pulitzer Prize for Drama, was a skeptic from an
early age. At age five, when her mother told her about
Santa Claus, Zona said, "You can't make me believe any
such stuff as that." When her mother told her that God

made bedtime, Zona said, "I don't believe it!" When her mother replied that God made people fall asleep, Zona retorted, "Then why am I sleepier when I go to church evenings than when I play hide-and-go-seek in the Brice's barn evenings?"

John Galsworthy

(1867–1933) | novelist, playwright

Galsworthy refused knighthood, gave away half of his fortune, and won the Nobel Prize for Literature in 1932. He co-founded with George Bernard Shaw the worldwide anti-censorship organization PEN International. Many of his writings dealt with social issues such as economic inequities, prison reform, marital rape, anti-Semitism, and mining strikes. "Humanism," he said, "is the creed of those who believe that, in the circle of enwrapping mystery, men's fates are in their own hands—a faith that for modern man is becoming the only possible faith."

Alice Hubbard

(1861–1915) | feminist writer

In the introduction to her book, *The American Bible*, a freethought work she edited, Alice Hubbard wrote: "This is the book we offer—a book written by Americans, for Americans. It is a book without myth, miracle, mystery, or metaphysics—a commonsense book for people who prize commonsense as a divine heritage. The book that will benefit most is the one that inspires men to think and to act for themselves." She said, "The world can only be redeemed through action—movement—motion. Uncoerced, unbribed and unbought, humanity will move toward the light." Alice and her husband, Elbert, tragically died on the *Lusitania*.

Zora Neale Hurston

(1891–1960) | author, folklorist, anthropologist
The daughter and granddaughter of Baptist preachers, Hurston wrote, "Prayer seems to me a cry of weakness, and an attempt to avoid, by trickery, the rules of the game as laid down. I do not choose to admit weakness. . . . It seems to me that organized creeds are collections of words around a wish. I feel no need for such." Writing about her religious upbringing, she said: "My head was full of misty fumes of doubt . . . Neither could I understand the passionate declarations of love for a being that nobody could see. Your family, your puppy and the new bull-calf, yes. But a spirit away off who found fault with everybody all the time, that was more than I could fathom."

Milan Kundera

(1929–) | novelist, resistance leader
Kundera lost his teaching post and saw his books banned when he became a leader of the resistance during the Soviet invasion of Czechoslovakia. "Totalitarianism is neither left nor right, and within its empire both will perish," he wrote. "I was never a believer, but after seeing Czech Catholics persecuted during the Stalinist terror, I felt the deepest solidarity with them. What separated us, the belief in God, was secondary to what united us. In Prague, they hanged the Socialists and the priests. Thus a fraternity of the hanged was born."

Ursula K. LeGuin

(1929–) | science fiction novelist

The author best known for her book *The Left Hand of Darkness* made her views on religion clear in the introduction to that novel: "I am an atheist." During her acceptance speech for the Emperor Has No Clothes Award given by the Freedom From Religion Foundation, she said:

> *People who spend their lives sewing doll clothes for a figment of their imagination have no business running a country, making laws, interfering in people's sex lives, teaching in public schools, or getting us into wars against people who make a different kind of doll clothes for a different figment of the imagination. Let the tailors of the garments of God sit in their tailor shops and stitch away, but let them stay there in their temples, out of government, out of the schools.*

James A. Michener

(1907–1997) | novelist

A Quaker by upbringing, the renowned historical novelist described his views this way:

> *I decided (after listening to a "talk radio" commentator who abused, vilified, and scorned every noble cause to which I had devoted my entire life) that I was both a Humanist and a liberal, each of the most dangerous and vilified type. I am a Humanist because I think humanity can, with constant moral guidance, create a reasonably decent society. I am terrified of restrictive religious doctrine, having learned from history that when men who adhere to any form of it are in control, common men like me are in peril. I do not believe that pure reason can solve the perceptual*

problems unless it is modified by poetry and art and social vision. So I am a Humanist. And if you want to charge me with being the most virulent kind—a secular humanist—I accept the accusation.

Samuel Porter Putnam

(1838–1896) | author, publisher, president—Freethought Federation of America

A former Congregationalist minister, then Unitarian, Putnam eventually broke with religion altogether and became "an open and avowed Freethinker." He wrote the opus *Four Hundred Years of Freethought*. His memoirs contain these words:

> *The last superstition of the human mind is the superstition that religion in itself is a good thing, though it might be free from dogma. I believe, however, that the religious feeling, as feeling, is wrong, and the civilized man will have nothing to do with it . . . [When the] shadow of religion disappeared forever . . . I felt that I was free from a disease.*

Elmina D. Slenker

(1827–1908) | birth control activist, journalist

The 19th-century freethinking feminist columnist was expelled from her Shaker family for becoming a "liberal." Originally a "sex hater," she changed her philosophy upon discovering that sex could be fun and thereafter advocated free sexual relations outside of marriage—as long as it did not include male-female genital intercourse. "When a mere girl," she said, "my mother offered me a dollar if I would read the Bible through; . . . despairing of reconciling many of its absurd statements with even my childish philosophy, . . . I became a sceptic, doubter, and unbeliever, long ere the 'Good Book' was ended."

Barbara Smoker

(1925–) | president—National Secular Society (U.K.), vice-president—Gay and Lesbian Humanist Association, author
Smoker was such a devout Catholic that she considered becoming a nun. Instead, she eventually renounced all religious faith and became president of the National Secular Society for 25 years. Her radio script, "Why I Am an Atheist," was broadcast on the BBC in 1985. In 1974, Smoker wrote: "People who believe in a divine creator, trying to live their lives in obedience to his supposed wishes and in expectation of a supposed eternal reward, are victims of the greatest confidence trick of all time."

John Steinbeck

(1902–1968) | novelist
Steinbeck wrote to his doctor near the end of his life: "Now finally, I am not religious so that I have no apprehension of a hereafter, either a hope or reward or a fear of punishment. It is not a matter of belief. It is what I feel to be true from my experience, observation, and simple tissue feeling." During his 1962 acceptance speech after winning the Nobel Prize for Literature, Steinbeck said:

> *We have usurped many of the powers we once ascribed to God. Fearful and unprepared, we have assumed lordship over the life or death of the whole world—of all living things. The danger and the glory and the choice rest finally in man. The test of his perfectibility is at hand. Having taken Godlike power, we must seek in ourselves for the*

responsibility and the wisdom we once prayed some deity might have. Man himself has become our greatest hazard and our only hope. So that today, St. John the apostle may well be paraphrased: In the end is the Word, and the Word is Man—and the Word is with Men.

James Thurber

(1894–1961) | humorist

Perhaps best known for his short story, "The Secret Life of Walter Mitty" (which spawned a 1947 movie starring Danny Kaye), the humorist and cartoonist was not a believer. "It is better to know some of the questions than all of the answers," Thurber said. "Thurber had never allowed his probing, restless mind to settle on any single theological insurance policy concerning the possibilities of the hereafter," wrote biographer Harrison Kinney. "He remained an agnostic."

John Toland

(1670–1722) | philosopher

The Irish writer was the first person to be called a "freethinker" (by Bishop George Berkeley), and the first "professional freecomposersthinker," according to the *Encyclopedia of Unbelief*. By age 15, he had rejected Roman Catholicism by his own reason. His more than 100 books, though worded carefully to avoid prosecution— the Irish House of Commons ordered one of his books burned, and one member even suggested that Toland himself should be burned—his rationalist writings were openly critical of religion.

Alice Walker

(1944–) | novelist, poet, civil rights activist

In *Anything We Love Can Be Saved*, Walker, a self-described "earthling" writes: "All people deserve to worship a God who also worships them. A God that made them, and likes them. That is why Nature, Mother Earth, is such a good choice. Never will Nature require that you cut off some part of your body to please It; never will Mother Earth find anything wrong with your natural way." In the chapter, "The Only Reason You Want to Go to Heaven Is That You Have Been Driven Out of Your Mind," Walker writes: "It is chilling to think that the same people who persecuted the wise women and men of Europe, its midwives and healers, then crossed the oceans to Africa and the Americas and tortured and enslaved, raped, impoverished, and eradicated the peaceful, Christ-like people they found. And that the blueprint from which they worked, and still work, was the Bible."

H. G. Wells

(1866–1946) | author

Best known as one of the pioneers of science fiction, Wells also wrote about history, politics, and social commentary, including his criticism of religion, *God the Invisible King*. Although he toyed briefly with the idea of a "divine will," it was a temporary aberration. He used his fame as an author to promote many causes, including the prevention of war. He wrote:

> *Indeed Christianity passes. Passes—it has gone! It has littered the beaches of life with churches, cathedrals, shrines*

*and crucifixes, prejudices and intolerances, like the sea
urchin and starfish and empty shells and lumps of sting-
ing jelly upon the sands here after a tide. A tidal wave
out of Egypt. And it has left a multitude of little wriggling
theologians and confessors and apologists hopping and
burrowing in the warm nutritious sand. But in the hearts
of living men, what remains of it now? Doubtful scraps of
Arianism. Phrases. Sentiments. Habits.*

Emile Zola

(1840–1902) | novelist

The famed French writer was an agnostic and a critic
of the Catholic Church and all forms of oppression. His
most enduring work is his open letter "J'Accuse," about
the Dreyfus case, in which he campaigned with Clemenceau to free the the French Jewish army officer falsely
accused of spying, and for which he was wrongly sentenced to prison. "When truth is buried underground,"
he said in that letter, "it grows, it chokes, it gathers such
an explosive force that on the day it bursts out, it blows
up everything with it . . . The truth is on the march, and
nothing shall stop it."

More writers' quotes about religion

"The kind of fraud which consists in daring to proclaim
the truth while mixing it with a large share of lies that
falsify it, is more widespread than is generally thought."
   —Marcel Proust

"When you once attribute effects to the will of a personal
God, you have let in a lot of little gods and evils—then
sprites, fairies, dryads, naiads, witches, ghosts and

goblins, for your imagination is reeling, riotous, drunk, afloat on the flotsam of superstition. What you know then doesn't count. You just believe, and the more you believe the more do you plume yourself that fear and faith are superior to science and seeing."
  —**Elbert Hubbard**

"I believe that when I am dead, I am dead. I believe that with my death I am just as much obliterated as the last mosquito you and I squashed."
  —**Jack London**

"There are a score of great religions in the world . . . and each is a mighty fortress of graft."
  —**Upton Sinclair**

"I read the Book of Job last night—I don't think God comes well out of it."
  —**Virginia Woolf**

"The Old Testament is responsible for more atheism, agnosticism, disbelief—call it what you will—than any book ever written; it has emptied more churches than all the counter-attractions of cinema, motor bicycle and golf course."
  —**A. A. Milne**

"It is, I think, an error to believe that there is any need of religion to make life seem worth living."
  —**Sinclair Lewis**

"Only Puritans think of the Devil as the most fascinating figure in the universe."
  —**Heywood C. Broun**

"To the absurd myths of God and an immortal soul, the modern world in its radical impotence has only succeeded in opposing the ridiculous myths of science and progress."
     —Andre Malraux

"I lead a perfectly healthy, satisfactory life without being religious. And I think more people should try it."
     —Peter Watson

"A few saints and a little charity don't make up for all the harm religion has done over the ages. . . . Religion has kept civilization back for hundreds of years, and the biggest mistake in the history of civilization, is ethical monotheism, the concept of the one God. Let's get rid of it and be rational."
     —Peter Watson

"One must choose between God and Man, and all 'radicals' and 'progressives,' from the mildest liberal to the most extreme anarchist, have in effect chosen Man."
     —George Orwell

"Man enjoys the great advantage of having a God endorse the codes he writes; and since man exercises a sovereign authority over woman, it is especially fortunate that this authority has been vested in him by the Supreme Being. For the Jews, Mohammedans, and the Christians, among others, man is master by divine right; the fear of God, therefore, will repress any impulse toward revolt in the downtrodden female."
     —Simone de Beauvoir

"When I told the people of Northern Ireland that I was an atheist, a woman in the audience stood up and said,

'Yes, but is it the God of the Catholics or the God of the Protestants in whom you don't believe?'"
    —Quentin Crisp

"Religion is the most malevolent of all mind viruses. We should get rid of it as quick as we can."
    —Arthur C. Clarke

"I was brought up a Catholic, became an agnostic, flirted with Islam and now hold a position which may be termed Manichee. I believe the wrong God is temporarily ruling the world and that the true God has gone under. Thus I am a pessimist but believe the world has much solace to offer: love, food, music, the immense variety of race and language, literature and the pleasure of artistic creation."
    —Anthony Burgess

"All gods from time immemorial are fantasies created by humans for the welfare of humans and to attempt to explain the seemingly inexplicable. But do we, in the third year of the 21st century of the Common Era and on the springboard of colonising the universe, need such palliatives? . . . Wherever one looks there is conflict: Protestants and Catholics in Northern Ireland; Jews, Christians and Muslims in Palestine; Muslims and Hindus in the Indian subcontinent; Christians and Muslims in Nigeria, Indonesia, Saudi Arabia and elsewhere. Is not the case for atheism made?"
    —Ludovic Kennedy

"I am an atheist (or at best a Unitarian who winds up in churches quite a lot)."
    —Kurt Vonnegut

"I regard monotheism as the greatest disaster ever to befall the human race. I see no good in Judaism, Christianity, or Islam."
  —Gore Vidal

"Christianity is such a silly religion."
  —Gore Vidal

"Being an atheist is a matter not of moral choice, but of human obligation."
  —John Fowles

"Christ died for our sins. Dare we make his martyrdom meaningless by not committing them?"
  —Jules Feiffer

"The very fears and guilts imposed by religious training are responsible for some of history's most brutal wars, crusades, pogroms, and persecutions, including five centuries of almost unimaginable terrorism under Europe's Inquisition and the unthinkably sadistic legal murder of nearly nine million women. History doesn't say much very good about God."
  —Barbara G. Walker

"I'm a nonbeliever. I don't believe in the existence of a God. I don't believe in the Christian dogma. I find it horrifyingly silly. The intolerance that flows from organized religion is the most dangerous thing on the planet."
  —Jane Rule

"When I started understanding how science works, it occurred to me that there just is no evidence that there is a God."
  —Ben Bova

"The tragedy is that every brain cell devoted to belief in the supernatural is a brain cell one cannot use to make life richer or easier or happier."
   —Kay Nolte Smith

"[My family is part of] the race of 'none,' [people] who do not believe, who do not carry on traditions. . . . In my parents' general view, new things were better than old, and the very fact that some ritual had been performed in the past was a good reason for abandoning it now. Because what was the past, as our forebears knew it? Nothing but poverty, superstition and grief. 'Think for yourself,' Dad used to say. 'Always ask why.'"
   —Barbara Ehrenreich

"In India, as elsewhere in our darkening world, religion is the poison in the blood. Where religion intervenes, mere innocence is no excuse. Yet we go on skating around this issue, speaking of religion in the fashionable language of 'respect.' What is there to respect in any of this, or in any of the crimes now being committed almost daily around the world in religion's dreaded name?"
   —Salman Rushdie

"I'm an atheist. I really don't believe for a moment that our moral sense comes from a God . . . It's human, universal, [it's] being able to think our way into the minds of others . . . people who do not have a sky god and don't have a set of supernatural beliefs assert their belief in moral values and in love and in the transcendence that they might experience in landscape or art or music or sculpture or whatever. Since they do not believe in

an afterlife, it makes them give more value to life itself. The little spark that we do have becomes all the more valuable when you can't be trading off any moments for eternity . . . I find that life is rich, diverse, fabulous, and extraordinary, conceived without a god."
—**Ian McEwan**

"When the whole world doesn't believe in God, it'll be a great place."
—**Philip Roth**

"I don't have any faith, but I have a lot of hope, and I have a lot of dreams of what we could do with our intelligence if we had the will and the leadership and the understanding of how we could take all of our intelligence and our resources and create a world for our kids that is hopeful."
—**Ann Druyan**

"We cannot be top country if we let science and education be run by people who think that dinosaurs drowned in Noah's flood."
—**Katha Pollitt**

"Gullibility and credulity are considered undesirable qualities in every department of human life—except religion . . . Why are we praised by godly men for surrendering our 'godly gift' of reason when we cross their mental thresholds? . . . Atheism strikes me as morally superior, as well as intellectually superior, to religion. Since it is obviously inconceivable that all religions can be right, the most reasonable conclusion is that they are all wrong."
—**Christopher Hitchens**

"The best way of defending atheists against defamation, it seems to me, is to employ good old rigorous argument, aggressively going after, for example, the flagrantly fallacious argument that without God there can be no morality."
   —Rebecca Newberger Goldstein

"If you describe yourself as 'Atheist,' some people will say, 'Don't you mean "Agnostic?"' I have to reply that I really do mean Atheist. I really do not believe that there is a god—in fact I am convinced that there is not a god (a subtle difference). I see not a shred of evidence to suggest that there is one. It's easier to say that I am a radical Atheist, just to signal that I really mean it, have thought about it a great deal, and that it's an opinion I hold seriously. It's funny how many people are genuinely surprised to hear a view expressed so strongly. In England we seem to have drifted from vague wishy-washy Anglicanism to vague wishy-washy Agnosticism—both of which I think betoken a desire not to have to think about things too much."
   —Douglas Adams

"Sure, I'm a soapbox atheist. But she [my daughter] doesn't have to take my word for anything. All she has to do is look around her, every day, to find the bible she needs—in the sky, sun, moon, Mars, leaves, lady bugs, stink bugs, possums, tadpoles, cardinals, the wonderful predatory praying mantises that have gotten really big and fat this year on all the insects this rainy year has brought. Life needs no introduction, explanation or excuse. Life is bigger than myth—except in California."
   —Natalie Angier

Composers (Classical)

"Religion has inspired such great music," we often hear. "Secular music doesn't compare." How can a person who does not believe in a Creator understand how to create beauty? If the purpose of life is to "glorify God," what is it that could possibly motivate a nonbeliever to write music? "Doesn't faith have the capacity to inspire people to great acts?" a student asked me during a debate on religion and society. "No atheists come to mind that have been important in the formation of classical or Romantic art or music."

John Philip Sousa, the "march king," agreed. He felt that "atheistic composers could not be inspired to great things." His own compositions came from a "higher power," he insisted. "The Unseen Helper sends me a musical idea, and that Somebody helps the public to lay hold of my meaning."* The belief that there is no purpose without God implies that there is no creativity without a Creator. A brief survey of the lives and views of some beloved composers will dispel the myth that only religion can inspire truly great music. If you have ever caught yourself humming one of their godless melodies— then you know that ain't necessarily so.

---

*Although Sousa did believe in God, he was not conventionally religious: "Inasmuch as Sousa did not attend church regularly in adulthood, especially while on the road, it would appear that he was not a religious man. He was, however, very much in tune with the Divine. Close friends often observed—quite accurately—that music was his religion. He sincerely believed that . . . a sermon could be preached with music as well as with words. . . . Specifically, he was Episcopalian, but his beliefs were broad. He believed in evolution . . . he put little stock in the literal interpretation of the Bible . . . he did not believe in the virgin birth." Bierley, Paul E., *John Philip Sousa: American Phenomenon*. Meredith Corporation, 1973. Page 103–103. "Unseen helper" quote from *Boston Post*, October 15, 1922, Bierley.

Ludwig van Beethoven

(1770–1827) | pianist, composer—nine symphonies, one opera, 23 piano sonatas

Beethoven was born into a Roman Catholic family. After working as an assistant organist, he studied in Vienna under Haydn. Beethoven was an admirer of Goethe, who rejected Christianity in favor of a pantheistic viewpoint. When his friend Moscheles returned a manuscript to Beethoven with the words "With God's help" written on it, Beethoven reportedly wrote in reply: "Man, help thyself." Biographer and friend Anton Schindler wrote that Beethoven was "inclined to Deism." Although, at the insistence of religious friends, he received Catholic ministrations near his death, Beethoven reportedly said in Latin, after the priest left: "Applaud, friends; the comedy is over." Biographer Sir George MacFarren described Beethoven as "a free thinker." According to Joseph McCabe, the *Catholic Encyclopedia* chose to omit Beethoven.

The *Ode to Joy,* in his Ninth Symphony, sets to music the humanistic words of Friedrich Schiller, artistically invoking pagan gods, not the god of the bible. The English translation, by the way, makes the lyrics more "Christian" than Schiller or Beethoven intended. "There is no record of his ever attending church service or observing the orthodoxy of his religion," writes George Marek. "He never went to confession. . . . Generally he viewed priests with mistrust."

"Beethoven was not a churchgoer and was suspicious of any sort of orthodoxy, religious or secular," writes Bill Cooke. "He composed very little religious

music, in the narrower sense of the term. His most
ostensibly religious piece was the *Missa solemnis* which
was . . . a hymn to Deism, and evokes the ideal not of
humanity managing to qualify for entrance into a distant
heaven above, but, in the words of Paul Griffiths, of a
'sovereign humanity in ultimate concord here on earth.' "

Hector Berlioz

(1803–1869) | *composer—best known:* Symphonie Fantastique,
Requiem

Identified with the French Romantic movement, the
mature Berlioz was impressed with religious form but
motivated by human passion. He acknowledged that
his earliest experiences with music were connected with
religious ritual, Christian as well as pagan. As a young
man, he briefly fell under the spell of the Catholic religion, "though his beliefs will not survive into adult life,"
according to biographer David Cairns. As a young composer, "when not copying parts (which he did 'till his
thumbs ached') he read the materialist philosophers and
physiologists whose works were in his physician father's
library—Locke, Cabanis, Gall—and found confirmation
for his own disbelief in a personal God," writes Cairns.
When he was 23, his unrequited love for the Irish Shake-
spearean actress Henrietta Smithson inspired his *Symphonie Fantastique*. She finally agreed to marry him after
she had attended a performance of the *Symphonie Fantastique* and realized that the work was his depiction of
his passionate love letters to her. This work was clearly
not motivated by a love for God—unless God is a red-
head. Cairns writes of the *Requiem* composed by Berlioz:

"Though it is not the work of an orthodox believer, it has Wordsworth's 'visionary gleam.' Berlioz spoke of himself as an atheist, at most as an agnostic. If he had a 'god,' it was Shakespeare: 'It is thou that art our father, our father in heaven, if there is a heaven,' he will cry out, in one of the most harrowing moments of his existence. But the very loss left a permanent mark." In a letter from Paris, on July 22, 1862, to Princess Sayn-Wittgenstein, Berlioz wrote: "Like you, I have one of the theological virtues, Charity; but unlike you, I have not the other two . . . [Hope and Faith]."

Georges Bizet

(1838–1875) | *pianist, composer—operas, best known:* Carmen
Georges Bizet, the French musical prodigy, entered the Paris Conservatoire at age nine. Over the next decade he won virtually every prize available, including the Prix de Rome. He refused a career as a concert pianist in order to compose operas. He wrote about 30, none particularly successful, until he composed *Carmen* in 1875, based on Prosper Merimee's book about a Spanish gypsy girl. *Carmen* was controversial not only because of its humble subject matter and passionate sweep, but because the libretto was written in French rather than the customary Italian, and (scandalously) could be understood by the audience. Criticism and a lukewarm reception closed the play after a brief run, although the composers of that day praised it.

Biographer William Dean writes that as a young man, struggling with his religious and philosophical views, Bizet was asked by his Academy to write a mass.

Preferring to write a comedy, he replied: "I don't want to write a mass before being in a state to do it well, that is a Christian. I have therefore taken a singular course to reconcile my ideas with the exigencies of Academy rules. They ask me for something religious: very well, I shall do something religious, but of the pagan religion. . . . I have always read the ancient pagans with infinite pleasure, while in Christian writers I find only system, egoism, intolerance, and a complete lack of artistic taste." Nine years later, he wrote: "Religion is a means of exploitation employed by the strong against the weak; religion is a cloak of ambition, injustice and vice . . . Truth breaks free, science is popularized, and religion totters; soon it will fall, in the course of centuries—that is, tomorrow. . . . In good time we shall only have to deal with reason."

Three months after the opening of *Carmen*, while the failed opera was still playing to empty houses, the dejected writer, who suffered from ill health, died of a heart attack at the age of 36, never knowing *Carmen* would become the best-known, best-loved, and most produced opera in history.

Johannes Brahms

(1833–1897) | pianist, composer—best known: "Brahms's Lullaby"

Brahms, the great German composer who was often called the "third B" (after Bach and Beethoven), had no faith in a god or religion. He was most often influenced by philosophy and literature and inspired by nature. "A great deal of his music," writes biographer Jan Swafford, "in its inspiration and spirit, rose from mountains and forests and open sky." Brahms occasionally used biblical texts, but only for artistic reasons. After the death of his mother, he wrote *Ein deutsches Requiem,* but selected only those words that relate to this life and to those who grieve, avoiding talk of eternal salvation. Noticing this secular spin, the conductor wrote to Brahms: "Forgive me, but I wondered if it might not be possible to extend the work in some way that would bring it closer to a Good Friday service . . . what is lacking, at least for a Christian consciousness, is the pivotal point: the salvation in the death of our Lord. . . ." But Brahms was not about to put up with that sort of thing. Even if the words come from the Bible, this was his response to death as a secular, skeptical, modern man. At the end of his Requiem, the dead are not reborn but released. When Brahms died, there was no death-bed conversion, no regret for having lived a godless life. His last words were to thank Artur Faber, father of the child for whom he had composed "Brahms's Lullaby," for the wine he brought that day.

Aaron Copland

(1900–1990) | conductor, composer—orchestral works, film scores, ballets, best known: Appalachian Spring, Rodeo, *"Fanfare for the Common Man"*

Aaron Copland was born into a well-off family of Jewish immigrants in New York City. "[A]lthough retaining strong memories of the music he heard in the synagogue and at Jewish weddings," Professor Howard Pollack writes:

> Copland evidenced little direct connection with Judaism or Jewish culture. He was neither religious nor observant. He

*rarely attended a synagogue service. In fact, in a 1974 let-
ter, he reminded a young friend that he had "resigned from
the Jewish church." . . . His friend and protégé, Leonard
Bernstein, would tease him by saying that he was not a
"real Jew." To all appearances, and by all accounts, he
was what many might call a secular humanist."*

Many critics, knowing Copland was from a Jewish
family, try to spot "prophetic statements" or "the Mosaic
voice" or "Hebraic ideas" in some of his compositions,
although we have no real evidence this was Copland's in-
tent. "All agreed that there was nothing explicitly Jewish
in the obvious sense . . . Yet there was something Jewish
in the musical style nonetheless," Botstein speculates of
Copland's music. Would these same critics, knowing that
Copland was also a homosexual, say that there is something "gay" in his musical style? The fact that an artist is
born into a religious family does not mean that the art is
therefore "religious."

Aaron Copland lived and died as a nonbeliever.
His will specified that his funeral service, if any, be
"non-religious."

Claude Debussy

*(1862–1918) | composer—best known: "Claire de Lune,"
"Prelude to the Afternoon of a Faun"*
French composer Claude Debussy, the originator of "musical impressionism," was a nonbeliever. His personal
views leaned toward a skeptical pantheism—if there is
a god, it is nature—but he rejected all creeds and had a
secular funeral. "I do not practise religion in accordance
with the sacred rites," he wrote.

I have made mysterious Nature my religion. I do not believe that a man is any nearer to God for being clad in priestly garments, nor that one place in a town is better adapted to meditation than another. When I gaze at a sunset sky and spend hours contemplating its marvelous ever-changing beauty, an extraordinary emotion overwhelms me. Nature in all its vastness is truthfully reflected in my sincere though feeble soul. Around me are the trees stretching up their branches to the skies, the perfumed flowers gladdening the meadow, the gentle grass-carpeted earth, . . . and my hands unconsciously assume an attitude of adoration. . . . To feel the supreme and moving beauty of the spectacle to which Nature invites her ephemeral guests! . . . that is what I call prayer.

Like other secular composers, Debussy sometimes utilized religious texts or stories. "Le Martyre de Saint-Sébastien" was an attempt to represent religious mysticism through music. The Archbishop of Paris, however, deemed the work "offensive to Christian consciences" and forbade Catholics from attending the performance. Protesting artistic censorship and defending the right of a nonbeliever to compose "religious" music, Debussy said:

Do you imagine that my works do not contain what I may call religious precedents? Do you propose to fetter the soul of the artist? Is it not obvious that a man who sees mystery in everything will be inevitably attracted to a religious subject? I do not wish to make a profession of faith. But, even if I am not a practicing Catholic nor a believer, it did not cost me much effort to rise to the mystical heights which the poet's drama attains. . . . I assure you that I wrote my music as though I had been asked to do it for a church. The result is decorative music, if you like, a noble

text interpreted in sounds and rhythms; and in the last
act when the saint ascends into Heaven I believe I have
expressed all the feelings aroused in me by the thought of
the Ascension. Have I succeeded? That no longer concerns
me. We have not the simple faith of other days.

Frederick Delius

(1862–1934) | composer—best known: Florida Suite,
On Hearing the First Cuckoo in Spring, Summer Night
on the River

A British-born composer of German descent, Fritz
("Frederick") Delius lived and worked in Florida, Virginia, France, Germany, and Norway. His first serious
work, *Florida Suite*, incorporated the sounds of plantation workers that he heard while working on his orange
plantation not far from Jacksonville as a young man. He
later studied at the Leipzig Conservatorium. Delius was
inspired by literature, nature, American Indians and
African Americans, the Florida landscape and European
mountains.

Delius was "a lifelong atheist," writes Lionel Carley.
He was "always ready to poke fun at the religious beliefs
of his friends." In a letter to Edvard Grieg, Delius wrote:
"I think the only improvement that Christ and Christianity have brought with them is Christmas. As people
really then think a little about others. Otherwise I feel
that he had better not have lived at all. The world has
not got any better, but worse & more hypocritical, & I
really believe that Christianity has produced an overall
submediocrity & really only taught people the meaning of
fear." Later in life, he wrote, "One thing is certain—that

English music will never be any good till they get rid of Jesus. Humanity is incredible. It will believe anything, anything to escape reality. I want to make myself very plain to you as regards religions and creeds. Personally, I have no use for any of them. There is only one real happiness in life, and that is the happiness of creating."

Edward Elgar

(1857–1934) | *composer—best known:* Pomp and Circumstance, Enigma Variations

Although born and raised in England as a believing Roman Catholic, composer Edward Elgar eventually discarded his faith toward the end of his life. Most of his works were religious in nature, although he would come to regret having written them. According to Professor Byron Adams, composer Frederick Delius reports that Elgar told him "it was a great pity that [Elgar] had wasted so much time and energy in writing those long-winded oratorios." Delius remarked to a friend that Elgar "might have been a great composer if he had thrown all that religious paraphernalia overboard."

Biographer Byron Adams wrote "The contradictory speculations advanced by the various authors that Elgar consulted, including such sceptics as Ernest Renan, may have caused only distress." In other words, reading the bible turned Elgar into an unbeliever. Elgar's loss of faith was not a defeat; it was a victory of reason over superstition. Elgar viewed composition as a natural exercise, claiming that he was trying to set the environment to music. All through his life, he used to sit outside and dream, and listen. Beneath a quotation from the "Woodland Interlude" from *Caractacus*, he wrote: ". . . This is what I hear all day—the trees are singing my music—or have I sung theirs? It is too beautiful here."

Wolfgang Amadeus Mozart

(1756–1791) | composer—operas, masses, ballets, more than 70 piano sonatas, 50 symphonies
The young Mozart was raised a believer, but he grew up to discard his faith. Son of a Catholic musician, the child prodigy conducted his first original Mass at age 12 in Vienna, was later made a Knight of the Golden Spur by the pope, and served as concertmaster to the Archbishop of Salzburg until, accused of neglecting his religion, he resigned the appointment in 1781. Mozart rejected many of his earlier religious views and joined the Freemasons, who required only a minimal belief in a deistic god and who were condemned by the Catholic Church. Although probably not an atheist, the mature Mozart had little use for religion. Referring to the orthodoxy of his youth, he said: "That is all over, and will never come back." He refused to ask for a priest when dying. His wife sent for one anyway, who declined to attend. He was buried in a pauper's grave, and nobody knows the exact location of his remains.

Niccolò Paganini

(1782–1840) | violin virtuoso, composer—best known: Caprice No. 24 in A minor
The great Italian violinist Niccolò Paganini composed his first sonata before the age of nine and made his first public appearance when he was eleven. He was ap-

pointed first violinist at the Lucca Court, where, reportedly practicing up to 15 hours a day, he became Europe's foremost violinist. Paganini's acclaimed six-year world tour—starting in Vienna and visiting major cities in Germany, Poland, Bohemia, England, and Ireland—wowed audiences with his legendary innovative technique and showmanship and made him a wealthy international celebrity. He played his own compositions, considered to be so diabolically intricate that some dazzled superstitious audience members widely accused him of having made a pact with the devil. Yet his tender passages routinely brought his listeners to tears. Paginini lived a religion-free life, refused the sacraments of the Roman Catholic church on his deathbed and any religious ritual at his burial. Even his religious biographer, Count Conestabili, admitted Paganini's "religious indifferentism."

Sergei Prokofiev

(1891–1953) | *composer—operas (*War and Peace*), ballets (*Romeo and Juliet*), children's music (*Peter and the Wolf*), film scores (*Alexander Nevsky*)*

Prokofiev gave up on the idea of religion at an early age. Biographer Harlow Robinson writes:

> *Neither of Prokofiev's parents was particularly religious. This was more surprising in his mother's case, since she came from a very devout peasant family, and her sisters were faithful churchgoers. His father came from the less religiously inclined merchant class, and his education at the university—oriented toward science and technology— did nothing to strengthen his faith in Russian Orthodoxy. Maria Grigorevna's natural skepticism and cynicism,*

*strengthened by the harsh reality of Russian provincial
life and her own family's struggles, led her eventually to
openly question and even mock church dogma, rather than
to embrace it. Prokofiev inherited these skeptical sentiments
from her. One should remember, too, that atheistic attitudes
were almost universal among the progressive intelligentsia
in Russia in the years leading up to the Revolution.*

"Generally speaking," Prokofiev said, "I was reserved in dealing with questions of the heart, and that trait showed up here, too; I waged the battle for religion internally, without sharing it or discussing it with anyone." After attending religious services with one of his aunts in a crowded, stuffy church smelling of incense, he fainted and had to be taken outside. "My fainting spell frightened me and cooled my desire for the church," he reported. "At home we didn't talk about religion. So, gradually the question faded away by itself and disappeared from the agenda. When I was 19, my father died; my response to his death was atheistic. The same was true when . . . I lost a close friend. . . . I took this 'farewell' very bitterly, the farewell of a human consciousness that had departed finally and forever."

Like so many other composers, Prokofiev died thinking about his music, making arrangements for the copying of a revision of the Fifth Piano Sonata and his last ballet, *The Stone Flower.* He died the same day as Josef Stalin—March 5, 1953—and had a small civil funeral accompanied by the music of his F Minor Sonata for Violin and Piano.

Maurice Ravel

(1875–1937) | *pianist, composer—best known:* Bolero, Pictures
at an Exhibition

"Although born of Catholic parents and baptized as an
infant," writes pianist and music professor Arbie Orenstein, "Ravel was not a practicing Catholic and did
not accept the last rites of the Church. He apparently
was an agnostic, relying upon his inner conscience and
moral sensitivity." Since he gave generously to charity and hated all forms of racism, his parish priest once
told him, "Monsieur Ravel, you are the most Christian
of my parishioners," even though Ravel called himself
an atheist. In a 1920 letter to his friend Ida Godebska,
Ravel wrote: "I spoke with Pierette Haour, an atheist like
myself, about what you had written concerning the benefits of religion," although another friend (Alexis Roland-
Manuel) seemed surprised at Ravel's self description and
claimed that he was "certainly not an atheist, but rather
a confirmed agnostic." Ravel's works contain a notable
absence of religious references and forms. He was most
commonly inspired by nature, fairy tales, folk songs, and
classical and oriental legends. He planned an opera about
Joan of Arc (never completed), but was not interested in
its religious significance: "I am thinking about Joan of
Arc. The famous novel of Delteil inspired me, and the
plan of the music is almost completed. . . . nature and
humanity, closely dependent, offer innumerable possibilities of musical interpretation."

When Ravel died, his body was interred at the cemetery of Levallois-Perret without religious ceremony.

Gioachino Rossini

(1792–1868) | composer—39 operas, best known: The Barber
of Seville, William Tell

Sometimes nicknamed "The Italian Mozart," Rossini
wrote instrumental music, chamber music, and sacred
music as well as the operas for which he is famous. The
overture to *William Tell* is one of the most famous and
most recorded pieces in history. In 1817 Rossini accepted the commission to write an opera based on Cinderella
(*La Cenerentola*) with the condition that all supernatural
elements be removed.

"Rossini was not at all devout," writes historian Gaia
Servadio. He often went through the conventional motions
of being a Catholic, though his true religion was music.
During his later years he wrote a mass, the *Petite Messe
solennelle*, which he jokingly called "the last sin of my old
age." As a prefatory note, he wrote a this dedication:

> *Dear God,*
> *Here it is finished, this poor little Mass. Is this sacred*
> *music that I have written or is it wicked music? I was bred*
> *for* opera buffa *as you know all too well. A little science,*
> *a little heart, that's all. Be blessed, then, and admit me to*
> *Paradise.*

It was a wonderfully humble, honest and secular way to
describe a life of art, or any good life, for that matter. Notice
that he did not add "a little faith."

"Rossini died a death he did not deserve," writes
Servadio. "The last rites were administered, a charade
which he—an agnostic if not an atheist—could have done
without. . . . He had been thinking of death for a quarter

of a century and was deeply offended that the cardinal failed to grasp that behind the mask there was another Rossini. He did not want to die in the hands of the Roman Catholic Church."

Robert Schumann

(1810–1856) | *pianist, composer—best known:* Scenes from a Childhood, Carnaval, Faust

German composer Robert Schumann's father was a bookseller who encouraged his young son to read the humanistic works of Schiller, Goethe, and many freethinkers, such as Byron. Schumann gave up Christian beliefs as a student. Schumann was educated at Leipzig and Heidelberg Universities for a law career. Unable to resist the pull of music, he first trained to be a pianist, then threw himself into composition. He founded the publication *Neue Zeitschrift fur Musik* in 1834, which he edited for 10 years, an influential contribution to the promotion of progressive thought on music. He married his beloved Clara Wieck, a talented concert pianist and composer, in 1840. During that year he composed 150 songs, many based on romantic tales. In 1841, he turned to orchestral music, in 1842 to chamber music, and in 1843 to choral music, including a secular oratorio and Goethe's *Faust*. His lieder set to music words by such freethinking writers as Goethe, Heine, and Kerner. Schumann had a devastating nervous breakdown, attended by hallucinations and suicidal impulses, in 1854. Although tended by Clara and his young protégé and friend Johannes Brahms, he did not recover and died in a sanitarium two years later. Writing about a goodbye walk Clara and

Brahms took with Schumann before checking him into a hospital toward the end of his life, biographer Jan Swafford notes: "Naturally they stopped at the Beethoven statue that Schumann had been visiting nearly every day; the monument was his church and his altar."

Richard Strauss

(1864–1949) | conductor, composer—tone poems, operas, best known: Also sprach Zarathustra, Salome

German composer Richard Strauss began piano lessons at four and musical composition by seven. He studied music and philosophy for two terms at Munich University and launched into a lifelong career as conductor. His tone poem *Also Sprach Zarathustra* ostensibly set to music Nietzsche's and his own nonreligious views, earning harsh criticism from the Church. His opera, *Salome* (1905), based on the play by Oscar Wilde, was a sensation not just because of the "blasphemous" subject matter, but because it was a musical stretch. He composed the Olympic Hymn for the 1936 games in Berlin. He was briefly appointed head of State Music (without his consultation) by the Third Reich. He was barred from working with his librettist, Stefan Zweig, who was Jewish, and it is believed he maintained silence about the Nazis in part because his grandchildren were part-Jewish. He received warnings about his private letters, which were screened by authorities. Strauss spent much of the war in Vienna, moving to Switzerland at the war's conclusion. He conducted for the final time when he turned 85. "[Strauss] did not believe in God, and he saw no spiritual dimension in his art," music critic Alex Ross wrote in

the *New Yorker*. At his funeral in Munich, there was no
Christian symbolism of any kind.

Giuseppe Verdi

(1813–1901) | *composer—operas, best known:* Riogoletto, La
Traviata, Aida

The great Italian composer Giuseppe Verdi was a hearty
skeptic, an altar boy who grew up to say: "Stay away
from priests." Biographer Mary Jane Phillips-Matz documents Verdi's "anticlericalism and refusal to believe
in God or any higher power." Instead of following the
Church, "he put his faith in land, gold, and his compositions." Verdi's wife, Giuseppina Strepponi, was
quite aware of his irreligious views. "For some virtuous
people," she wrote of him, "a belief in God is necessary.
Others, equally perfect, while observing every precept of
the highest moral code, are happier believing in nothing." She also wrote:

> He is a jewel among honest men; he understands and feels
> himself every delicate and elevated sentiment. And yet this
> brigand permits himself to be, I won't say an atheist, but
> certainly very little of a believer, and that with an obstinacy
> and calm that make me want to beat him. I exhaust myself
> in speaking to him about the marvels of the heavens, the
> earth, the sea, etc. It's a waste of breath! He laughs in my
> face and freezes me in the midst of my oratorical periods
> and my divine enthusiasm by saying "you're all crazy,"
> and unfortunately he says it with good faith.

If atheism is the lack of belief in a god, then Verdi
was indeed an atheist. He was certainly at least agnostic. He avoided writing ecclesiastical music and was an

anti-Papist and a rationalist. At the end of his successful career, Verdi shared his wealth, endowing the city of
Milan with two million lira in 1898 to establish a home
for aging musicians. Twenty-eight thousand mourners
showed up for his nonreligious funeral, which, according
to his request, was conducted without "any part of the
customary formulae."

Ralph Vaughan Williams

*(1872–1958) | composer—operas, ballets, symphonies, hymn
arrangements, film scores*
"There is no reason why an atheist could not write a
good Mass," Ralph (pronounced "Rafe") Vaughan Williams said. Indeed, the prolific British composer who
helped compile *The English Hymnal* and who wrote
religious music that is performed in liturgies and worship
services around the world was himself not a believer. His
wife, Ursula, wrote of Ralph:

> *Although a declared agnostic, he was able, all through his
> life, to set to music words in the accepted terms of Chris-
> tian revelation as if they meant to him what they must
> have meant to George Herbert or to Bunyan . . . He was
> an atheist during his later years at Charterhouse and at
> Cambridge, though he later drifted into a cheerful agnosti-
> cism: he was never a professing Christian . . . This attitude
> did not affect his love of the authorized version of the Bible.
> The beauty of the idiom of the Jacobean English was estab-
> lished in his mind long before he went away to school and,
> like the music of Bach, remained as one of his essential
> companions through life. He was far too deeply absorbed
> by music to feel any need of religious observance.*

Ralph's grandmother was a sister of Charles Darwin.
As a child, he spent considerable time in his famous uncle's home in Down. Learning about *The Origin of Species,*
he asked his mother what it was about. She answered:
"The Bible says that God made the world in six days,
Great Uncle Charles thinks it took longer: but we need not
worry about it, for it is equally wonderful either way."

At Cambridge, Ralph spent more time with music
than religious duties. "In those days attendance at chapel
was compulsory," Ursula writes, "and one morning
when Ralph's absence had been noted he was sent for
by authority":

> *"I did not see you in chapel this morning, Mr. Vaughan
> Williams."*
> *"No, sir."*
> *"Perhaps, however, you were in the organ loft?"*
> *"Yes, sir, I was."*
> *"Well, you can pray as well in the organ loft as in any
> other part of the chapel."*
> *"Yes, Sir—but I didn't."*

Feminists

If purpose comes from solving problems, then the 19th- and
20th-century feminists were and are a purposeful lot. Many
of those women and men, especially the leaders, were nonbelievers, and that makes perfect sense. It is the church, the
bible, and religion, after all, that have been mainly responsible for holding women back from full participation in the
world. Annie Laurie Gaylor, a lifelong active feminist herself,
researched and chronicled the lives of more than 50 of those

women in her massive work *Women Without Superstition: "No God—No Masters."* She shows that those leaders and thinkers did not consider equality, fairness, and freedom to be simply nice goals to strive for, "woman's work" like planting a garden or baking cookies; they are essential conditions for a full life.

It is difficult to imagine that when the phrase "liberty and justice for all" was written, the words "for all" did not include half the population. Women could not vote or run for public office. In the 19th century, women could not go to college. They did not own their own paychecks. They had no legal say over the fate of their children. They lived under a system of "civil death." In spite of the lofty words of freedom and democracy spoken by the founding fathers of the United States, the full "pursuit of happiness" was available only to men. No women were at the Constitutional Convention. Not only could women not be involved as leaders, but, just like in the Catholic Church, they could not even vote for their leaders. Reading history, it is almost as if women were invisible. But they were there, and they cared, though the only muffled influence they could muster was from a distance, from outside the walls of Constitution Hall, as when Abigail Adams bravely suggested to her husband to "remember the ladies."

Women Without Superstition takes almost 800 pages to describe the rich and active lives of many of these women. They were not just disgruntled critics of religion. Their lives were filled with the purpose of correcting inequality. I only have space to list some of them here. Most of the women who led the fight to correct this injustice were nonbelievers, infidels, skeptics, or religiously unorthodox rebels. Who would dare say any of their lives lacked purpose?

Ayaan Hirsi Ali

(1969–) | *Somali immigrant, member of the Dutch Parliament*
Ali, who now works globally for women's rights, writes
in her book *Infidel*:

> *I had left God behind years ago. I was an atheist. . . .*
> *From now on I could step firmly on the ground that was*
> *under my feet and navigate based on my own reason and*
> *self-respect. My moral compass was within myself, not in*
> *the pages of a sacred book. . . . All life is problem solving*
> *. . . There are no absolutes; progress comes through critical*
> *thought. . . . Reason, not obedience, should guide our lives.*
> *Though it took centuries to crumble, the entire ossified cage*
> *of European social hierarchy—from kings to serfs, and be-*
> *tween men and women, all of it shored up by the Catholic*
> *Church—was destroyed by this thought.*

Susan B. Anthony

(1820–1906) | *women's rights activist*
Less outspoken about religion than some activists, Susan
B. Anthony confined her many public speeches to the
issue of women's voting rights and avoided all mention
of religion. "But while I do not consider it my duty," she
wrote, "to tear to tatters the lingering skeletons of the old
superstitions and bigotries, yet I rejoice to see them crum-
bling on every side." She was an agnostic who went to the
Unitarian Church but openly professed that her "creed"
was "the perfect equality of women." Stanton said of
Anthony: "Every energy of her soul is centered upon the
needs of *this* world. To her, work is worship." Although
in more recent times some evangelical-based right-to-life

groups have held her up as an anti-abortion icon, her writings actually contain not a single pro-life statement.

Emily Cape

(1865–1953) | sociologist

Emily Cape apparently was the first woman student admitted to Columbian University (now George Washington University), and she later studied sociology with Professor Lester Ward, who is sometimes called the father of American sociology. "Like Professor Ward, she is an Agnostic and an ardent humanitarian," wrote historian Joseph McCabe. Cape founded a School of Sociology in New York. Traveling the world and noticing some "ignorant" priests on the ship, she wrote: "No wonder their 'flocks' are 'low in education.' "

Anne Nicol Gaylor

(1926–) | founder and first president of the Freedom From Religion Foundation

In the early 1970s, Gaylor started the Women's Medical Fund, the longest-lived continuously operating abortion charity in the country. "Nothing fails like prayer," Gaylor says, agreeing with Robert G. Ingersoll that "the hands that help are better far than lips that pray." The words inscribed on the annual freethought sign at the Wisconsin State Capitol building were written by Anne Gaylor: "At this season of the Winter Solstice, let reason prevail. There are no gods, no devils, no angels, no heaven or hell. There is only our natural world. Religion is but myth and superstition that hardens hearts and enslaves minds."

Harriet Martineau

(1802–1876) | sociologist

British author Harriet Martineau, who blazed a trail for women by supporting herself entirely by writing (including 50 books and more than 1,600 articles in her own name), is credited by some historians as being the "first sociologist." Her book Society in America was as famous as Alexis de Tocqueville's writings about America. She especially examined the status of American women, whom she found unhealthily obsessed with religion. Offering children an alternative to "pernicious superstition," Harriet wrote Household Education in 1848 as a secular guide for parents. "There is no theory of a God, of an author of Nature, of an origin of the Universe, which is not utterly repugnant to my faculties," she wrote.

Margaret Sanger

(1879–1966) | founder of Planned Parenthood

The woman most responsible for the availability of birth control in the United States was arrested many times for distributing obscene material. She jumped bail and fled to exile in Europe, where she observed Dutch birth control clinics and ultimately returned to the U.S. to start her own. The motto for her newsletter, the *Woman Rebel*, was "No Gods—No Masters." She charged that her prosecutions were an effort by church leaders to keep women in a state of submission and accused the Catholic Church of insensitivity to women's needs.

Elizabeth Cady Stanton

(1815–1902) | founder of the women's movement

The woman who first proposed amending the U.S. Constitution to recognize the votes of women at the historic 1848 Seneca Falls Convention and who dedicated more than 50 years of her life to women's rights died 18 years before the amendment became reality, but her efforts ultimately won out. Universal suffrage was eventually ratified in 1920 as the 19th Amendment to the U.S. Constitution: "The right of citizens of the United States to vote shall not be denied or abridged by the United States or by any State on account of sex."

Stanton was not just a passive nonbeliever. She was outspokenly critical of religion. Her first letter to Susan B. Anthony, who would become a lifetime co-worker in the cause, contained the words, "The Church is a terrible engine of oppression, especially as concerns woman." Later in life, looking back on years of activism, she wrote, "In the early days of woman-suffrage agitation, I saw that the greatest obstacle we had to overcome was the bible. It was hurled at us on every side."

Stanton could hardly make a speech or write an article without condemning the sexism in religion. In "The Degraded Status of Women in the Bible," she wrote:

> *I have endeavored to dissipate these religious superstitions from the minds of women, and base their faith on science and reason, where I found for myself at least that peace and comfort I could never find in the bible and the church . . . the less they believe, the better for their own happiness and development. . . . For fifty years the women of this nation have tried to dam up this deadly stream that poisons*

all their lives, but thus far they have lacked the insight or courage to follow it back to its source and there strike the blow at the fountain of all tyranny, religious superstition, priestly power, and the canon law.

Frances Wright
(1795–1852) | feminist, abolitionist

Earlier in the 19th century, the first woman to publicly lecture in the United States was Scottish-born feminist and abolitionist Frances Wright. "Turn your churches into halls of science," she said. "Exchange your teachers of faith for expounders of nature . . . Fill the vacuum of your mind!" In her 1828 speech, "Divisions of Knowledge," she said: "I am not going to question your opinions. I am not going to meddle with your belief. I am not going to dictate to you mine. All that I say is, examine, inquire. Look into the nature of things. Search out the grounds of your opinions, the for and the against. Know why you believe, understand what you believe, and possess a reason for the faith that is in you." She founded and published the *Free Inquirer* newspaper and established a communal school near Memphis, Tennessee, to educate runaway slaves.

More feminists' quotes about religion

"Give me truth; cheat me by no illusion."
    —**Margaret Fuller**

"Do you tell me that the Bible is against our rights? Then I say that our claims do not rest upon a book written no one knows when, or by whom. Do you tell me what Paul or Peter says on the subject? Then again I reply that our claims do not rest on the opinions of any one, not even on those of Paul and Peter, . . . Books and opinions, no matter from whom they came, if they are in opposition to human rights, are nothing but dead letters."

—Ernestine L. Rose

"During the ages, no rebellion has been of like importance with that of Woman against the tyranny of the Church and State; none has had its far reaching effects. We note its beginning; its progress will overthrow every existing form of these institutions; its end will be a regenerated world."

—Matilda Joslyn Gage

"It is impossible to exaggerate the evil work theology has done in the world."

—Lydia Maria Child

"The being cannot be termed rational or virtuous who obeys any authority but that of reason."

—Mary Wollstonecraft

"Every denial of education, every refusal of advantages to women, may be traced to this dogma [of original sin], which first began to spread its baleful influence with the rise of the power of the priesthood and the corruption of the early Church."

—Lillie Devereux Blake

"If your Bible is an argument for the degradation of woman, and the abuse by whipping of little children, I advise you to put it away, and use your common sense instead."

—Lucy Colman

"I rejoice that I played my part in that educating of
England which has made impossible for evermore the
crude superstitions of the past, and the repetition of
the cruelties and injustices under which preceding
heretics suffered."
   —Annie Besant

"The abominable laws respecting [women in the Bible]
. . . are a disgrace to civilization and English literature;
and any family which permits such a volume to lie on
their parlor-table ought to be ostracized from all respectable society."
   —Ella E. Gibson

"A religious person is a dangerous person. He may not
become a thief or a murderer, but he is liable to become
a nuisance. He carries with him many foolish and harm-
ful superstitions, and he is possessed with the notion
that it is his duty to give these superstitions to others.
That is what makes trouble. Nothing is so worthless
as superstition."
   —Marilla M. Ricker

"Is not the Church today a masculine hierarchy, with a
female constituency, which holds woman in Bible lands
in silence and in subjection? No institution in modern
civilization is so tyrannical and so unjust to woman as
is the Christian Church. It demands everything from her
and gives her nothing in return."
   —Josephine K. Henry

"I do not know of any divine commands. I do know of most important human ones. I do not know the needs of a god or of another world. . . . I do know that women make shirts for seventy cents a dozen in this one. I do know that the needs of humanity and this world are infinite, unending, constant, and immediate. They will take all our time, our strength, our love, and our thoughts; and our work here will be only then begun."
   —Helen H. Gardener

"The question of souls is old—we demand our bodies, now. We are tired of promises, god is deaf, and his church is our worst enemy."
   —Voltairine de Cleyre

"Preach about yesterday, Preacher! . . . Preach about the other man, Preacher!/ Not about me!"
   —Charlotte Perkins Gilman

"I have to admit that one of my favorite fantasies is that next Sunday not one single woman, in any country of the world, will go to church. If women simply stop giving our time and energy to the institutions that oppress, they would have to cease to do so."
   —Sonia Johnson

"It's an incredible con job, when you think of it, to believe something now in exchange for life after death. Even corporations, with all their reward systems, don't try to make it posthumous."
   —Gloria Steinem

Human Rights Activists

Of course, we should not ignore the other half of the human race when considering fighters for human rights.

I had the pleasure of touring Cameroon with Norm Allen, where we both lectured at a freethought conference in 2007. Norm, an outspoken happy atheist and humanist, is the director of African American Humanists at the Center for Inquiry, editor of the periodical African American Humanists, and editor of the books, *African American Humanism: An Anthology* and *The Black Humanist Experience: An Alternative to Religion*. Those books include contributions from many humanists (not necessarily all atheists) and nonbelievers.

Stephen Pearl Andrews

(1812–1886) | *abolitionist*

Attorney Andrews was mobbed and almost killed when he agitated to make Texas a free state. A polyglot who spoke more than 30 languages, Andrews was considered the leading Chinese language scholar in the United States. He was a regular contributor to the freethought newspaper, *The Truth Seeker*. An advocate of unconventional philosophies, he promoted a movement called universology, became a founding father of the sect of spiritualism, and coined the term "scientology" (unrelated to the modern cult of the same name).

Moncure Daniel Conway

(1832–1907) | *abolitionist*

A law school dropout, Conway was ordained as a Methodist minister, then attended Harvard divinity school and joined the Unitarian clergy. He soon broke with that church over his abolitionist views and became an agnostic. He helped dozens of his father's slaves escape at the start of the Civil War. His scholarly works include *The Life of Paine*, a biography of Nathaniel Hawthorne, and *Demonology and Devil Lore*. London's Conway Hall, where freethought lectures continue to this day, was named for him. In his autobiography, Conway wrote:

> *Sunday was a day of just so much external restraint as public opinion absolutely demanded. I learned at last, as I came to be about seventeen, that my father was an entire freethinker, as much as I am now. It shocked me much, because he never taught me anything, allowed me to pick up religion from any one around me, and then scolded me because I embraced beliefs which he knew must condemn him. I think this neglect to be honest with children is a terrible evil. I have lost years of thought, and wandered wide and done such unwise conceited things, and encountered risks for soul and body, all of which might have been obviated by his frank teaching.*

Frederick Douglass

(1818 [?]–1895) | abolitionist, author, editor
At that 1848 Seneca Falls Convention, Douglass, who was born a slave, was the only man who spoke in favor of Elizabeth Cady Stanton's call for suffrage. Douglass became a famous abolitionist, author, editor, and outspoken critic of slavery, often at great personal risk. He was nominated for vice-president to run with Victoria Woodhull in 1872 for the Equal Rights Party. Douglas became a U.S. marshal of the District of Columbia and was later appointed minister resident and consul-general to Haiti. Although

probably not an atheist, Douglass sometimes revealed his freethought sentiments: "I prayed for twenty years but received no answer until I prayed with my legs," Douglas wrote in his autobiography.

W.E.B. Du Bois

(1868–1963) | civil rights activist

A founder of the National Association for the Advancement of Colored People, Du Bois was known as the "father of pan-Africanism." In his autobiography, he wrote:

> By the time of graduation I was still a "believer" in orthodox religion, but had strong questions which were encouraged at Harvard. In Germany I became a freethinker and when I came to teach at an orthodox Methodist Negro school I was soon regarded with suspicion, especially when I refused to lead the students in public prayer. When I became head of a department at Atlanta, the engagement was held up because again I balked at leading in prayer, . . . I flatly refused again to join any church or sign any church creed. From my 30th year on I have increasingly regarded the church as an institution which defended such evils as slavery, color caste, exploitation of labor and war. I think the greatest gift of the Soviet Union to modern civilization was the dethronement of the clergy and the refusal to let religion be taught in the public schools.

Lloyd Garrison

(1805–1879) | journalist, abolitionist

An early abolitionist/suffragist, Garrison was especially harsh in his criticism of the church's complicity with slavery. At the fifth national woman's suffrage convention in Philadelphia in 1854, Garrison pointed out that

the most determined opposition [suffrage] encounters is
from the clergy generally, whose teachings of the Bible are
intensely inimical to the equality of woman with man.
. . . Why go to the Bible [about women's suffrage]? What
question was ever settled by the Bible? What question of
theology or any other department? . . . The human mind is
greater than any book. The mind sits in judgment on every
book. If there be truth in the book, we take it; if error, we
discard it . . . In this country, the Bible has been used to
support slavery and capital punishment; while in the old
countries, it has been quoted to sustain all manner of tyr-
anny and persecution. All reforms are anti-Bible.

James Russell Lowell

(1819–1891) | abolitionist poet

A Harvard-educated lawyer and the son of a Unitarian
minister, Lowell was an ardent abolitionist and became
an agnostic later in life. He was the first editor of the
Atlantic Monthly, later edited the *North American Re-*
view, taught at Harvard for almost 20 years, and was
an international diplomat. "Toward no crimes have men
shown themselves so cold-bloodedly cruel as in punish-
ing differences of belief," Lowell wrote.

Journalists

The "fourth estate," in order to be an effective and objective
check and balance, functions best when it is most critical of
the powers that be, whether political or religious. For journal-
ists, purpose in life comes from solving the problems of how
to gain accurate information and how best to communicate
it to the world. In the United States, the same constitutional

amendment that guarantees freedom of religion also guarantees freedom of the press.

Ambrose Bierce

(1842–1913 [?]) | journalist, satirist
Bierce fought in the Civil War and later wrote more than 90 novels based on his experiences. He worked as a journalist for several newspapers, and was eventually hired by William Randolph Hearst in 1887, producing a column of witty epigrams, many of which are collected in *The Devil's Dictionary*:

> *Faith, n. Belief without evidence in what is told by one who speaks without knowledge, of things without parallel.*

> *Camels and Christians receive their burdens kneeling.*

> *Pray. v. To ask that the laws of the universe be annulled in behalf of a single petitioner, confessedly unworthy.*

> *Christian, n. One who believes that the New Testament is a divinely inspired book admirably suited to the spiritual needs of his neighbor. One who follows the teachings of Christ insofar as they are not inconsistent with a life of sin.*

> *Infidel, n. In New York, one who does not believe in the Christian religion; in Constantinople, one who does.*

Bierce disappeared in Mexico while covering the 1913 revolution and was never seen or heard from again.

Anatole France

(1844–1924) | journalist, poet, novelist
Despite a Catholic school education, France became an outspoken atheist known for his anticlericalism. He won

the Nobel Prize in Literature in 1921. "The thoughts of the gods," he wrote, "are not more unchangeable than those of the men who interpret them," he wrote. "They advance—but they always lag behind the thoughts of men. . . . The Christian God was once a Jew. Now he is an anti-Semite."

Michael Kinsley
(1951–) | *journalist, TV pundit, online journal editor*
Kinsley, who wrote for *Time*, the *Los Angeles Times*, the *Washington Post*, the *New Republic*, *Harpers*, and *The Economist*, and hosted *Crossfire* for six years, wrote:

> *As a devout believer, [Gen.] Boykin may also wonder why it is impermissible to say that the God you believe in is superior to the God you don't believe in. I wonder this same thing as a nonbeliever: Doesn't one religion's gospel logically preclude the others'? (Except, of course, where they overlap with universal precepts, such as not murdering people, that even we nonbelievers can wrap our heads around.)*

H. L. Mencken
(1880–1956) | *journalist, satirist*
America's most prominent iconoclastic journalist, known as the Sage of Baltimore, was famed for his coverage of the 1925 Scopes "monkey trial" over the teaching of evolution in schools. He wrote 28 books, including *In Defense of Women* and *Treatise of the Gods*. Although his father was agnostic, his Lutheran mother sent him to Sunday School, which he later defined as, "A prison in which children do penance for the evil conscience of their parents." Mencken worked most of his adult life

at the *Baltimore Sun*, where he produced many of his famous aphorisms in the column "The Free Lance":

> *Faith may be defined briefly as an illogical belief in the occurrence of the improbable.*

> *Puritanism: The haunting fear that someone, somewhere may be happy.*

> *Sunday: A day given over by Americans to wishing that they themselves were dead and in Heaven, and that their neighbors were dead and in Hell.*

> *Theology: An effort to explain the unknowable by putting it into terms of the not worth knowing.*

> *I believe that religion, generally speaking, has been a curse to mankind—that its modest and greatly overestimated services on the ethical side have been more than overcome by the damage it has done to clear and honest thinking . . . I believe that it is better to tell the truth than to lie. I believe that it is better to be free than to be a slave. And I believe that it is better to know than be ignorant.*

Robin Morgan

(1941–) | feminist author, poet, journalist, editor, lecturer, organizer, activist

As a child actor in the 1950s, Morgan played Dagmar on the popular TV series *Mama*. She left show biz to write, and became a founder and leader of the contemporary feminist movement. She was editor in chief of *Ms.* for four years and is now its International consulting editor. She is a cofounder of the Feminist Women's Health Network, the Feminist Writers' Guild, Media Women, and the National Network of Rape Crisis Centers. Her book *The Demon Lover: On the Sexuality of Terrorism* tells the personal story of her travel to refugee camps in the Middle East, with a post-9/11 introduction and afterword. Bemoaning the state of religion in the United States, she wrote, "the Founders must be picketing in their graves. They were a mix of freethinkers, atheists, Christians, agnostics, Freemasons and Deists. . . . the Founders were, after all, revolutionaries. Their passion— especially regarding secularism—glows in the documents they forged and in their personal words."

Ron Reagan

(1958–) | TV pundit

The son of President Ronald Reagan and Nancy Reagan stopped going to church when he was 12. He joined the Joffrey Ballet Company as a corps de ballet dancer. Since 1983 he has worked as a broadcast and print journalist and television and radio host. Reagan serves on the Advisory Board of the Creative Coalition, a nonpartisan group that mobilizes entertainers and artists for causes such as First Amendment rights, arts advocacy, and public education. Along with his mother, Reagan has been a strong supporter of embryonic stem cell research. In 2004, the *New York Times* asked him if he'd like to be president. "I would be unelectable," Reagan said. "I'm an atheist. As we all know, that is something people won't accept." That same year he accepted the Freedom From Religion Foundation's Emperor Has No Clothes Award, saying,

> *Religions may persist, but they come and they go. Where are the old Norse gods today? Where are the worshippers of Amon-Ra today? A thousand years from now, what will*

people make of a man tortured to death on a cross, of a
prophet who was said to ride a white horse up to a mythi-
cal heaven? What will our distant progeny think of claims
by some that they have a special exclusive compact with
a deity? . . . I can't read the future, certainly. But I am
certain of one thing: reason. Reason and freethought will
remain a hallmark of the human species. The ability of hu-
man beings to gaze out at the wondrous, baffling universe
in which we find ourselves, with minds uncluttered by
dogma, has been and always will be the measure of our
success. Faith will fade, religions will flower and vanish,
but reason remains.

Andy Rooney

(1919–) | television commentator, author

The award-winning commentator, who became a famous
fixture on CBS News's *60 Minutes*, does not believe in
God, saying, "We all ought to understand we're on our
own. Believing in Santa Claus doesn't do kids any harm
for a few years but it isn't smart for them to continue
waiting all their lives for him to come down the chim-
ney with something wonderful. Santa Claus and God are
cousins. . . . I'd be more willing to accept religion, even
if I didn't believe it, if I thought it made people nicer
to each other but I don't think it does." Often avoiding
questions about his own beliefs even while satirizing
the church, Rooney said in his 1999 book *Sincerely,*
Andy Rooney that he was an agnostic. Later, during a
2004 debate about the film *The Passion of the Christ*, he
asserted that he was actually an atheist. He was awarded
the 2001 Emperor Has No Clothes award by the Freedom From Religion Foundation.

George Seldes

(1890–1995) | *investigative journalist*

A World War I combat correspondent, Seldes went on to become an international reporter for the *Chicago Tribune* and spent the next ten years in postrevolutionary Russia, Mussolini's Italy, and Mexico. Blacklisted as a communist in the McCarthy era, he was unable to get his articles published in periodicals, and he went on to write 21 books. He was the first to report the link between cancer and cigarette smoking. In his autobiography, *Witness to a Century,* Seldes wrote:

> *And so [my brother] Gilbert and I, brought up without a formal religion, remained throughout our lifetimes just what Father was, freethinkers. And, likewise, doubters and dissenters and perhaps Utopians. Father's rule had been "Question everything, take nothing for granted," and I never outlived it, and I would suggest it be made the motto of a world journalists' association.*

Louis "Studs" Terkel

(1912–2008) | *author, historian, radio broadcaster*

Studs Terkel's Chicago-based talk radio show ran for 45 years, during which he also wrote 18 books about American history and current affairs. At age 93, he became the oldest person ever to receive a successful heart transplant. In a radio interview, Terkel declared, "I'm an agnostic. . . . You asked about the afterlife. Well, I can't take bets on it. Who's going to take my bet, you know? I, myself, don't believe in any afterlife. I do believe in this life, and what you do in this life is what it's all about."

To one National Public Radio interviewer, he defined "agnostic" as "a cowardly atheist."

Performing Artists

Jimmy Cliff

(1948–) | Reggae musician

Cliff, known as the "Father of Reggae Music," is the only living musician to hold the Jamaican Order of Merit. Cliff says he has "graduated from religion." When asked by Stephen Colbert, "[When you die] which scorecard do you want to be graded on? Christian, Jew, Muslim?" Cliff answered: "On the scorecard of truth and facts."

Isadora Duncan

(1887–1927) | dancer

When Isadora Duncan, who would become known as the originator of modern dance, was five years old, her teacher told her that Santa Claus had brought candies and cakes as a special treat. When Isadora responded, "I don't believe lies!" she was kicked out of the class. At home, her mother reassured her: "There is no Santa Claus and there is no God, only your own spirit to help you." Especially admired in Europe, inspired by literature, and influenced by intellectuals and freethinking friends, such as atheist composer Ralph Vaughan Williams, Isadora's godless life was free and unconventional.

Tom Lehrer

(1928–) | songwriter, satirist, mathematics professor
Tom Lehrer, whose song "The Vatican Rag" is a perennial hit with freethinkers, said: "I firmly believe all religion is bullshit, but I don't think I would have gone and written a song expressing that, unless I could figure out a way to make it funny."

John Lennon

(1940–1980) | singer-songwriter, musician
Though Lennon was confirmed in the Anglican Church during childhood and fellow Beatles Paul McCartney and George Harrison were raised Catholic, all the Beatles declared themselves atheists in a 1965 *Playboy* magazine interview. The following year, band co-founder John Lennon sparked one of the biggest music scandals of all time when he declared in a press conference that "Christianity will go. It will vanish and shrink. I needn't argue with that; I'm right and I will be proved right. We're more popular than Jesus now. I don't know which will go first—rock and roll or Christianity. Jesus was all right, but his disciples were thick and ordinary. It's them twisting it that ruins it for me." The remark sparked protests across the American Bible Belt, including Beatles records being nailed to crosses and burned by the Ku Klux Klan. In an apology to the Pope, Lennon explained, "I'm sorry I opened my mouth. I'm not anti-God or anti-religion. I wasn't knocking it or putting it down. I was just saying it as a fact, and it's true . . ."

Lennon and his fellow Beatles experimented with various belief systems in the coming years, most notably the Hindu-influenced Trancendental Meditation of Maharishi Mahesh Yogi, whose association with the Beatles made the guru world-famous. But in the wake of several sex scandals between the Maharishi and his female followers, Lennon left in disgust and wrote several songs about it, including "Sexy Sadie."

Lennon became less and less religious before his death. Talking about his dalliance with Buddhism, he said: ". . . [T]his whole religion business suffers from the 'Onward, Christian Soldiers' bit. There's too much talk about soldiers and marching and converting. I'm not pushing Buddhism, because I'm no more a Buddhist than I am a Christian; but there's one thing I admire about the religion: There's no proselytizing." In the song "God," which Yoko Ono said was most representative of his views, Lennon wrote: "God is a concept by which we can measure our pain. . . I don't believe in magic, I don't believe in I-ching, I don't believe in bible . . . I don't believe in Jesus . . . I don't believe in Buddha . . . I just believe in me, Yoko and me, and that's reality."

David Randolph

(1914–2010) | conductor—best known: Handel's Messiah

Some composers and critics insist that there is no such thing as religious music. So said David Randolph, the famed conductor who performed Handel's *Messiah*, one of the most widely known pieces of "religious" music, before audiences 170 times—although he himself did not believe in any religion. He wrote,

> *We find that music, by itself, without benefit of a text, cannot reveal whether its intentions are sacred or secular, and*

117

the emotions evoked by the music—exultation, excitement,
joy, sadness, and so forth—cannot be identified as either
sacred or secular in origin. The devotional frame of mind
with which many listeners hear the overture to Messiah
stems from their knowledge of the fact that it is part of a
work whose text is on a sacred subject.

Much "religious" music was originally written for
secular purposes and later adapted to a religious text.
Randolph, who at age 94 became the oldest conductor
ever to perform at Carnegie Hall, wrote, "An outstanding example is the chorus 'For unto us a Child is born,'
in Handel's *Messiah*. This music, despite the sacred
atmosphere now associated with it, was originally a love
duet composed to the Italian words *"No, di voi non vo*
fidarmi, cieco Amor, crudel beltà" ("No, I no longer wish
to trust you, blind love, cruel beauty.") Randolph's book,
This Is Music: A Guide to the Pleasures of Listening, is
an insightful and useful introduction to music apprecia-
tion, stripping away many of the lofty "meanings" that
so many professional critics pretend to notice, that we
mere listeners are supposedly unable to grasp. "No series
of notes," he wrote, "can be demonstrated to contain, in
itself, a religious thought or sentiment, just as none can
be proven to be, per se, irreligious. All music is organized
sound. All music is made up of the same ingredients. The
difference lies in the ways in which they are organized."

Think of the melody to "Onward, Christian Soldiers,"
written by Arthur S. Sullivan of Gilbert & Sullivan fame.
If I didn't know the words to this hymn, written in a style
similar to Sullivan's comic tunes of pomposity and buf-
foonery, I could imagine it fitting quite well into *Pirates*

of Penzance ("Modern Major General") or *Mikado* ("Behold the Lord High Executioner"). Taken seriously—and Sullivan indeed wrote serious music, including hymns— "Onward, Christian Soldiers" betrays a chilling, intolerant, dangerous militaristic face of religion; but perhaps if we nonbelievers can pretend he was writing "tongue in cheek," as he did with Gilbert, we can hear the song as the very model of a major mythic comedy.

Eddie Vedder

(1964–) | *singer-songwriter*

When asked his feelings about God, singer and lyricist Eddie Vedder told Janeane Garofalo in 1998:

> *I think it's like a movie that was way too popular. It's a story that's been told too many times and just doesn't mean anything. Man lived on the planet—[placing his fingers an inch apart], this is 5,000 years of semi-recorded history. And God and the Bible, that came in somewhere around the middle, maybe 2,000. This is the last 2,000, this is what we're about to celebrate [indicating about ¼ of an inch]. Now, humans, in some shape or form, have been on the earth for three million years [pointing across the room]. So, all this time, from there to here, there was no God, there was no story, there was no myth and people lived on this planet and they wandered and they gathered and they did all these things. The planet was never threatened. How did they survive for all this time without this belief in God? I'd like to ask this to someone who knows about Christianity and maybe you do. That just seems funny to me. . . . That laws are made and wars occur because of this story that was written, again, in this small part of time.*

More performing artists' quotes about religion

"I don't believe in marriage in the conventional way," he told Larry King. "I am not religious person, and marriage in front of altar wouldn't say anything to me."
    —**Mikhail Baryshnikov**

"I'm an atheist. . . . how unfortunate it is to assign responsibility to the higher up for justice amongst people."
    —**Ani DiFranco**

"From my point of view, I would ban religion completely. The reality is that organized religion doesn't seem to work. It turns people into hateful lemmings and it's not really compassionate."
    —**Elton John**

"If ever I'm asked if I'm religious I always reply, 'Yes, I'm a devout musician.' Music puts me in touch with something beyond the intellect, something otherworldly, something sacred."
    —**Sting**

Playwrights and Screenwriters

Of course, actors would have nothing to say if it were not for those who write the plays and movies. Over the centuries, they have proven to be an outspoken lot.

Edward Albee

(1928–) | playwright

Albee won three Pulitzer Prizes for his plays *A Delicate Balance*, *Seascape*, and *Three Tall Women*, as well as the Tony and Obie awards. He called himself a "nominal Quaker" because he admired the sect's pacifism, but did not believe in God. One of his most famous plays, *Who's Afraid of Virginia Woolf*, was inspired by his experiences as an undergraduate student at Trinity College, from which he was expelled for refusing to attend mandatory chapel services. In that play, the character Martha says, "I swear to *God* George, if you even *existed* I'd divorce you."

Ingmar Bergman

(1918–2007) | film director, producer, screenwriter

The legendary Swedish filmmaker wrote in his autobiography:

> *I have struggled all my life with a tormented and joyless relationship with God. Faith and lack of faith, punishment, grace, and rejection, all were real to me, all were imperative. My prayers stank of anguish, entreaty, trust, loathing, and despair. God spoke, God said nothing . . . No one is safe from religious ideas and confessional phenomena . . . We can fall victim to them when we least expect it. It's like Mao's flu, or being struck by lightning . . . You were born without purpose, you live without meaning, living is its own meaning. When you die, you are extinguished. From being you will be transformed to non-being. A god does not necessarily dwell among our capricious atoms.*

Bjornstjerne Bjornson

(1832–1910) | novelist, director, playwright, poet
Though less known than Ibsen today, this Norwegian
author's plays were the first Norwegian works to be performed outside Scandinavia. He won the Nobel Laureate
in Literature in 1903. Next to Ibsen in acclaim, Bjornson
became "an aggressive Agnostic," according to Joseph Mc-
Cabe, after reading British Freethinker Herbert Spencer.

Georg Buchner

(1813–1837) | playwright
When this German author died at the age of 23, he had
already built a solid reputation as a powerful writer. In
1923, Buchner's hometown of Darmstadt created the
Georg Buchner Prize for literature, which is still one of
the most prestigious awards in the country. In the play
Danton's Death, the character Payne (modeled after
Thomas Paine), says: "First you adduce morality as a
proof of God, and then cite God in support of morality.
You reason in a beautiful circle, like a dog biting his
own tail."

Rupert Hughes

*(1872–1956) | film director, composer, president of the
American Writers Association*
The uncle of tycoon Howard Hughes, Rupert did not
believe in God. Explaining why he quit going to church,
he said it was

> *because I came to believe that what is preached in the
> churches is mainly untrue and unimportant, tiresome,
> hostile to genuine progress, and in general not worth-*

*while. . . . As for those who protest that I am robbing
people of the great comfort and consolation they gain from
Christianity, I can only say that Christianity includes hell,
eternal torture for the vast majority of humanity, for most
of your relatives and friends. Christianity includes a devil
who is really more powerful than God, and who keeps
gathering into his furnaces most of the creatures whom
God turns out and for whom he sent his son to the cross in
vain. If I could feel that I had robbed anybody of his faith
in hell, I should not be ashamed or regretful.*

Henrik Ibsen

(1828–1906) | playwright, director

Ibsen's social criticism led him to grow more passionate
as an unbeliever as the years passed. The protagonist of
his play *The Emperor and the Galilean* sets out to overthrow Christianity. "With pleasure I will torpedo the
ark," he wrote. "Bigger things than the State will fall, all
religion will fall."

Christopher Marlowe

(1564–1593) | playwright, poet

William Shakespeare's chief rival, Marlowe was derided
as an atheist by some of his political enemies. In the play
Dr. Faustus, the character Faustus proclaims, "Hell's a fable," and in the play *Tamburlaine the Great*, the protagonist burns the Koran and challenges Muhammad to "work
a miracle." Accused of denying the divinity of Christ,
Marlowe was threatened with prosecution for heresy.

Moliere

(1622–1673) | actor, playwright

The irreverent comic playwright (whose offstage name
was Jean Baptiste Poquelin) was threatened with being
burned alive for his scandalous views, and the Catholic
Church banned the performance of his plays. In *Tartuffe*,
he was forced to change the character of a hypocritical
priest to a nonreligious role. A monologue by Cleante,
another character in that play, contains these words:

> *There is nothing, I think, so odious as the whitewashed out-
> side of a specious zeal; as those downright imposters, those
> bigots whose sacrilegious and deceitful grimaces impose on
> others with impunity, and who trifle as they like with all
> that mankind holds sacred; those men who, wholly given to
> mercenary ends, trade upon godliness, and would purchase
> honour and reputation at the cost of hypocritical looks and
> affected groans; who, seized with strange ardour, make use
> of the next world to secure their fortune in this; who, with
> great affectation and many prayers, daily preach solitude
> and retirement while they themselves live at Court; who
> know how to reconcile their zeal with their vices; who are
> passionate, revengeful, faithless, full of deceit, and who, to
> work the destruction of a fellow-man, insolently cover their
> fierce resentment with the cause of Heaven.*

Upon his death, by special dispensation from the
King of France, Moliere was given a secret funeral at
night and buried in a "non-sacred" area of the church
cemetery reserved for unbaptized infants.

Eugene O'Neill

(1888–1953) | *playwright*

Though educated in Catholic boarding schools, the playwright, who later won the Nobel Prize for Literature and four Pulitzer Prizes, was persuaded away from his religious beliefs by his friend, John Reed, founder of the Communist Labor Party. O'Neill told his second wife, "When I'm dying, don't let a priest or Protestant minister or Salvation Army captain near me. Let me die in dignity. Keep it as simple and brief as possible. No fuss, no man of God there. If there is a God, I'll see him and we'll talk things over."

George Bernard Shaw

(1856–1950) | *playwright*

The only writer ever to win both the Nobel Prize for Literature and an Academy Award for Best Screenplay (for *Pygmalion*), Shaw co-founded, along with atheists Graham Wallas and Beatrice and Sydney Webb, the London School of Economics to promote "the betterment of society." Although he started calling himself a mystic in the 1890s—after having said he became an atheist at the age of ten—this did not damper his rational criticism of religion. "It is not disbelief that is dangerous to society, it is belief," he wrote in 1912. "There is nothing in religion but fiction," he wrote in 1924. "The fact that a believer is happier than a sceptic is no more to the point than the fact than a drunken man is happier than a sober one. The happiness of credulity is a cheap and dangerous quality of happiness, and by no means a necessity of life. Whether Socrates got as much out of life as Wesley

[John Wesley, founder of Methodism] is an unanswer-
able question; but a nation of Socrateses would be much
safer and happier than a nation of Wesleys. . . . At all
events, it is in the Socratic man and not in the Wesleyan
that our hope lies now." In his last will and testament,
Shaw wrote that his "religious convictions and scientific
views cannot at present be more specifically defined than
as those of a believer in creative revolution." He also
requested that no memorial to him should "take the form
of a cross or any other instrument of torture or symbol of
blood sacrifice."

Voltaire

(1694–1778) | playwright, novelist, philosopher
Francois-Marie Arouet, better known by the pen name
Voltaire, was a leader of the Age of Enlightenment who
openly satirized religion. His *Lettres philosophiques*
galvanized French reform—his publisher was sent to the
Bastille, the book sentenced to be "torn and burned in
the Palace," while Voltaire escaped Paris. After the devastating Lisbon earthquake of 1755, which killed 15,000
and injured as many more, Voltaire wrote: "But how
conceive a God supremely good/ Who heaps his favours
on the sons he loves,/ Yet scatters evil with as large a
hand?" He wrote to Frederick the Great, "Christianity is
the most ridiculous, the most absurd, and bloody religion
that has ever infected the world." After the first edition
of Voltaire's *Philosophical Dictionary* sold out, Geneva
officials had the books burned, as did officials in Holland
and Paris. In that book, Voltaire wrote: "Atheism is the
vice of a few intelligent people . . . There are no sects

in geometry . . . The truths of religion are never so well understood as by those who have lost the power of reasoning . . . Sect and error are synonymous . . . Common sense is not so common."

Oscar Wilde

(1854–1900) | *playwright, novelist, bon vivante*
A celebrated playwright and novelist—as well as lifelong skeptic who often toyed with joining one church or another but never did—Wilde fell from grace in London social circles after suing his lover for libeling him by claiming he was a homosexual. The defense proved that the claim was true, and Wilde was sentenced to two years' hard labor for the "crime" of gross indecency. He was a master of epigrams:

> *I think that God in creating Man somewhat overestimated his ability.*

> *The only way to get rid of a temptation is to yield to it.*

> *He hasn't a single redeeming vice.*

> *A thing is not necessarily true because a man dies for it.*

> *Truth, in matters of religion, is simply the opinion that has survived.*

> *There is no sin except stupidity.*

> *Science is the record of dead religions.*

Under medical duress, five days before he died of syphilitic meningitis, Wilde was conditionally baptized into the Catholic Church, though there is some question whether he was conscious at the time.

More playwrights' and screenwriters' quotes about religion

"I'm simply a nonbeliever and have been forever. . . . I'm interested in saying, 'Let us discuss the existential question. We are all going to die, that is the end of all consciousness. There is no afterlife. There is no God. Now what do we do.' That's the point where it starts getting interesting to me. . . . [I am] not just an atheist, but a total nonbeliever."
   —David Cronenberg

"Technically, I'm an agnostic, but I definitely believe in hell—especially after watching the fall TV schedule."
   —Matt Groening

"The whole idea of god is absurd. If anything, *2001* shows that what some people call 'god' is simply an acceptable term for their ignorance. What they don't understand, they call 'god' . . . I chose to do Dr. Clarke's story as a film because it highlights a critical factor necessary for human evolution; that is, beyond our present condition. This film is a rejection of the notion that there is a god; isn't that obvious?"
   —Stanley Kubrick

"Thank God, I'm still an atheist."
   —Luis Buñuel

When asked by *The Onion* magazine, "Do you believe in God?" Oscar-winning filmmaker Steven Soderbergh made this comprehensive and thoughtful reply: "No."

Philanthropists

Andrew Carnegie

(1835–1919) | tycoon, philanthropist

Andrew Carnegie wrote in his autobiography: "Not only had I got rid of the theology and the supernatural, but I had found the truth of evolution." In a letter to a friend, Carnegie wrote:

> *The whole scheme of Christian Salvation is diabolical as revealed by the creeds. An angry God, imagine such a creator of the universe. Angry at what he knew was coming and was himself responsible for. Then he sets himself about to beget a son, in order that the child should beg him to forgive the Sinner. This however he cannot or will not do. He must punish somebody—so the son offers himself up & our creator punishes the innocent youth, never heard of before—for the guilty and became reconciled to us. . . . I decline to accept Salvation from such a fiend.*

In another letter, Carnegie wrote: "More and more I realize we should think less & less of 'Heaven our Home!' more & more of 'Home our Heaven.' "

Bill Gates

(1955–) | entrepreneur

Microsoft founder Bill Gates, one of the wealthiest people in the world, is also one of the most generous philanthropists. *Time* magazine named him one of the 100 people who most influenced the 20th century. The Bill and Melinda Gates Foundation is the largest transparently operated charity (as opposed to a religious charity) in the world, having given dozens of billions of dollars to meet real human needs that are often ignored by governments. When asked if there is something special, perhaps divine, about the human soul, Gates replied, "I don't have any evidence on that." In the same interview, he said, "Just in terms of allocation of time resources, religion is not very efficient. There's a lot more I could be doing on a Sunday morning."

Stephen Girard

(1750–1831) | revolutionary American philanthropist
The wealthy ship owner Stephen Girard, considered the richest man in America when he died, was a great philanthropist and a nonbeliever. He personally saved the U.S. government from financial collapse during the War of 1812. Girard not only contributed to many charities and endowed schools and colleges (and founded Girard College), but he rolled up his sleeves and personally worked as a nurse during the Philadelphia yellow fever outbreak in 1793. In the terms for the endowment of money for a college for orphans, Girard stipulated:

> *I enjoin and require that no ecclesiastic, missionary, or minister of any sect whatever shall ever hold or exercise any station or duty whatever in the said college; nor shall any such person ever be admitted for any purpose, or as a visitor, within the premises appropriated to the purpose of the said college. . . . My desire is that all the instructors and teachers in the college shall take pains to instill into the minds of the scholars the purest principles of morality, so that, on their entrance into active life, they may, from inclination and habit, evince benevolence toward their fel-*

low creatures, and u love of truth, sobriety, and industry,
adopting at the same time such religious tenets as their
matured reason may enable them to prefer.

Philosophers

The human drive to "figure it all out" has motivated many of
the great thinkers. Philosophy, the "love of wisdom," broke
away from theology precisely because religion is conservative,
limiting ideas to a narrow range of established "truth." There
can be no true purpose in life without the ability to think freely.

Pierre Bayle

(1647–1706) | philosopher
The French philosopher who became known as the "father of the Enlightenment" said, "No nations are more
warlike than those which profess Christianity." After
experimenting with a forced conversion to Catholicism,
he recanted from the faith, jokingly calling himself a "literal Protestant" because he protested everything. Bayle
was the first to argue for complete religious toleration
and freedom of conscience, including for Jews, Muslims,
and atheists. "It is pure illusion to think that an opinion
which passes down from century to century to century,
from generation to generation, may not be entirely false."

Auguste Comte

(1798–1857) | philosopher, sociologist
Rejecting belief in God by age 14, Comte conceived a
"Religion of Humanity," which did not find a wide fol-
lowing, and was the founder of Positivism: "The law is

131

this: that each of our leading conceptions—each branch of our knowledge—passes successively through three different theoretical conditions: the Theological, or fictitious; the Metaphysical, or abstract; and the Scientific, or positive." He is also considered to be the "father" of sociology. "All good intellects have repeated, since Bacon's time, that there can be no real knowledge but which is based on observed facts."

Nicolas de Condorcet

(1743–1794) | *mathematician, philosopher*

The Marquis de Condorcet was one of the atheists that Thomas Jefferson said were "known to have been among the most virtuous of men." He was a social and educational reformer, a champion of women's rights and of minority rights. After the French Revolution, the marquis was entrusted with drafting a new constitution for the country, but a dispute with the French National Convention caused him to flee for his life and go into hiding. He died mysteriously, but not before finishing the *Sketch for a Historical Picture of the Progress of the Human Mind* in 1794. An optimist who believed in progress, Condorcet wrote: "Our hopes for the future condition of the human race can be subsumed under three important heads: the abolition of inequality between nations, the progress of equality within each nation, and the true perfection of mankind." Speaking to the future—a message we still need to hear today—Condorcet said:

> But even if we agree that the limit will one day arrive,
> nothing follows from it that is in the least alarming as far
> as either the happiness of the human race or its indefi-

132

*nitc perfectibility is concerned, if we consider that, before
all this comes to pass, the progress of reason will have
kept pace with that of the sciences, and that the absurd
prejudices of superstition will have ceased to corrupt and
degrade the moral code by its harsh doctrines instead of
purifying and elevating it, we can assume that by then
men will know that, if they have a duty towards those who
are not yet born, that duty is not to give them existence
but to give them happiness; their aim should be to promote
the general welfare of the human race or of the society
in which they live or of the family to which they belong,
rather than foolishly to encumber the world with useless
and wretched beings.*

Thomas Hobbes

(1588–1679) | *philosopher, author*

When Hobbes wrote his works, a charge of atheism was
punishable by death. His freethinking books were blamed
by believers for the Great Plague of 1665 and the Great
Fire of 1666. His work helped give birth to the enlightenment. Hobbes was at minimum a rationalist deist, if
not an atheist. In *Leviathan*, which Parliament targeted
as "heresy," Hobbes wrote:

*Seeing there are no signs nor fruit of religion but in man
only, there is no cause to doubt but that the seed of religion
is also only in man . . . Fear of power invisible, feigned
by the mind or imagined from tales publicly allowed,
RELIGION; not allowed, SUPERSTITION. . . . They that
approve a private opinion, call it opinion; but they that
mislike it, heresy; and yet heresy signifies no more than
private opinion.*

Baron d'Holbach

(1723–1789) | *philosopher, encyclopedist*

Arguably the most passionate atheist of the Enlightenment, the baron wrote: "Religion is a mere castle in the air. Theology is ignorance of natural causes; a tissue of fallacies and contradictions." An optimist, he predicted: "If the ignorance of nature gave birth to the gods, knowledge of nature is destined to destroy them." In *Common Sense*, he observed:

> *In all parts of our globe, fanatics have cut each other's throats, publicly burnt each other, committed without a scruple and even as a duty, the greatest crimes, and shed torrents of blood . . . We find, in all the religions, "a God of armies," a "jealous God," an "avenging God," a "destroying God," a "God," who is pleased with carnage, and whom his worshippers consider it a duty to serve . . . How could the human mind progress, while tormented with frightful phantoms, and guided by men, interested in perpetuating its ignorance and fears? Man has been forced to vegetate in his primitive stupidity: he has been taught stories about invisible powers upon whom his happiness was supposed to depend. Occupied solely by his fears, and by unintelligible reveries, he has always been at the mercy of priests, who have reserved to themselves the right of thinking for him, and of directing his actions.*

David Hume

(1711–1776) | *philosopher, historian*

Raised as a strict Calvinist, Hume rejected religion in his writings, but in quite ambiguous terms to avoid prosecution for infidelity. Many of his writings on the subject were not published until after his death. He wrote: "Examine the religious principles which have, in fact, prevailed in the world, and you will scarcely be persuaded that they are anything but sick men's dreams." In the same work, Hume called the god of the Calvinists "a most cruel, unjust, partial and fantastical being. The Christian religion not only was at first attended with miracles, but even at this day cannot be believed by any reasonable person without one."

John Stuart Mill

(1806–1873) | philosopher, member of Parliament (U.K.)
Mill remembered that his agnostic father

> *impressed upon me from the first, that the manner in which the world came into existence was a subject on which nothing was known: that the question, "Who made me?" cannot be answered, because we have no experience or authentic information from which to answer it; and that any answer only throws the difficulty a step further back, since the question immediately presents itself, Who made God?*

Mills called Christianity "essentially a doctrine of passive obedience; it inculcates submission to all authorities found established." Not a complete atheist, Mills was comfortable with a non-supernatural "limited liability" deism, but admired the skeptics: "The world would be astonished if it knew how great a proportion of its brightest ornaments—of those most distinguished even in popular estimation for wisdom and virtue—are complete skeptics in religion."

Jean Jacques Rousseau

(1712–1778) | *philosopher, writer*

A deist, Rousseau was less radical about religion than his friends Diderot and d'Holbach but was still persecuted for his irreverent views. His book *The Social Contract*, which introduced the motto *"Liberte, egalite, fraternite,"* contains this denunciation: "Christianity preaches only servitude and dependence. Its spirit is so favorable to tyranny that it always profits by such a regime. True Christians are made to be slaves, and they know it and do not much mind: this short life counts for too little in their eyes."

Bertrand Russell

(1872–1970) | *philosopher, mathematician, historian, pacifist*

Alongside his many accomplishments in diverse other fields, which led to a Nobel Peace Prize for Literature, Russell was an ardent peace activist. During a 1953 BBC radio broadcast, he said: "Cruel men believe in a cruel God and use their belief to excuse their cruelty. Only kindly men believe in a kindly God, and they would be kindly in any case." In *Why I Am Not A Christian*, he wrote: "I believe that when I die I shall rot, and nothing of my ego will survive. I am not young, and I love life. But I should scorn to shiver with terror at the thought of annihilation. Happiness is nonetheless true happiness because it must come to an end, nor do thought and love lose their value because they are not everlasting."

George Santayana

(1863–1952) | philosopher, poet, novelist

Although the Spanish expatriate philosopher called himself an "aesthetic Catholic," he was an agnostic skeptical naturalist who did not shy away from criticizing religion: "Christianity persecuted, tortured, and burned. Like a hound it tracked the very scent of heresy. It kindled wars, and nursed furious hatreds and ambitions. It sanctified, quite like Mohammedanism, extermination and tyranny."

Jean-Paul Sartre

(1905–1980) | philosopher, playwright, novelist

Part of the French Resistance during World War II, Sartre was twice the target of terrorist bomb attacks. He later headed the International War Crimes Tribunal. His existentialist writings were pointedly atheistic: "Illusion has been smashed to bits; martyrdom, salvation and immortality are falling to pieces; the edifice is going to rack and ruin; I collared the Holy Ghost in the basement and threw him out." To *Life* magazine, he said: "We have lost religion, but we have gained humanism."

Peter Singer

(1946–) | philosopher, animal-rights advocate

It is interesting that the man who is considered the world's leading ethicist is also an atheist. Peter Singer said: "Atheists and agnostics do not behave less morally than religious believers, even if their virtuous acts rest on different principles. Non-believers often have as strong and sound a sense of right and wrong as anyone, and have worked to abolish slavery and contributed to other efforts to alleviate human suffering." Accepting the Emperor Has No Clothes Award from the Freedom From Religion Foundation, Singer said:

> *If I claim that there are fairies in the bottom of my gar-*
> *den and that they tell me to do certain things, or that I've*
> *been visited by aliens or whatever else there might be,*
> *you might want some evidence. I think we should regard*
> *claims about the existence of God or about the divinity of*
> *Jesus as exactly similar. In the absence of evidence, nobody*
> *should really believe these claims . . . Once you give up*
> *standards of reasoning and of using evidence for your be-*
> *liefs, anything is possible, including a belief that it's a good*
> *thing to fly aeroplanes full of people into office buildings*
> *full of more people, and that somehow that will lead to you*
> *being rewarded in an afterlife. That's why I think it's time*
> *to take the offensive on this sort of belief.*

Benedict (Baruch) Spinoza
(1632–1677) | philosopher

Although considered an atheist by his critics, Spinoza was a deist, at most a pantheist, a skeptical philosopher who rejected immortality and miracles. Bertrand Russell called him "the noblest and most lovable of the great philosophers." Trained as a rabbi, Spinoza left Judaism: "I do not know how to teach philosophy without becoming a disturber of established religion." In his book on ethics, Spinoza wrote, "True virtue is life under the direction of reason." In *Tractatus Theologico-Politicus*, he said "Philosophy has no end in view save truth; faith looks for nothing but obedience and piety."

Henry David Thoreau

(1817–1862) | *author, naturalist*

In his book *On Civil Disobedience,* Thoreau wrote: "Your church is a baby-house made of blocks." In a journal, he noted that it is appropriate for a church to be the ugliest building in a village "because it is the one in which human nature stoops to the lowest and is the most disgraced." In his diary, Thoreau disapproved of the attempt to convert Native Americans "from their own superstitions to new ones." When he was dying, he refused to talk about religion, saying, "One world at a time."

More philosophers' quotes about religion

"Wandering in a vast forest at night, I have only a faint light to guide me. A stranger appears and says to me: 'My friend, you should blow out your candle in order to find your way more clearly.' This stranger is a theologian."

— **Denis Diderot**

"No power of government ought to be employed in the endeavor to establish any system or article of belief on the subject of religion . . . in no instance has a system in regard to religion been ever established, but for the purpose, as well as with the effect of its being made an instrument of intimidation, corruption, and delusion, for the support of depredation and oppression in the hands of governments."

— **Jeremy Bentham**

"All religions promise a reward for excellences of the will or heart, but none for excellences of the head or understanding."
   —**Arthur Schopenhauer**

"Religion has been compelled by science to give up one after another of its dogmas, of those assumed cognitions which it could not substantiate."
   —**Herbert Spencer**

"There is not sufficient love and goodness in the world to permit us to give some of it away to imaginary beings."
   —**Friedrich Nietzsche**

"When we hear the ancient bells growling on a Sunday morning we ask ourselves: Is it really possible! This, for a Jew, crucified two thousand years ago, who said he was God's son?"
   —**Friedrich Nietzsche**

"A god who begets children with a mortal woman; a sage who bids men work no more, have no more courts, but look for the signs of the impending end of the world; a justice that accepts the innocent as a vicarious sacrifice; someone who orders his disciples to drink his blood; prayers for miraculous interventions; sins perpetrated against a god, atoned for by a god; fear of a beyond to which death is the portal; the form of the cross as a symbol in a time that no longer knows the function and ignominy of the cross—how ghoulishly all this touches us, as if from the tomb of a primeval past! Can one believe that such things are still believed?"
   —**Friedrich Nietzsche**

"After coming into contact with a religious man, I always feel I must wash my hands."
  —**Friedrich Nietzsche**

"Those who are not religious have available to them a rich ethical outlook, all the richer indeed for being the result of reflection as opposed to convention, whose roots lie in classical antiquity when the great tradition of ethical thought in Western philosophy began."
  —**A. C. Grayling**

"Science is the great antidote to the poison of enthusiasm and superstition."
  —**Adam Smith**

"Intellectually, religious emotions are not creative but conservative. They attach themselves readily to the current view of the world and consecrate it."
  —**John Dewey**

"If faith cannot be reconciled with rational thinking, it has to be eliminated as an anachronistic remnant of earlier stages of culture and replaced by science dealing with facts and theories which are intelligible and can be validated."
  —**Erich Fromm**

"The facts on which the true believer bases his conclusions must not be derived from his experience or observation but from holy writ . . . To rely on the evidence of the senses and of reason is heresy and treason. . . . Thus the effectiveness of a doctrine should not be judged by its profundity, sublimity or the validity of the truths it embodies, but by how thoroughly it insulates the individual from his self and the world as it is. What Pascal said of an effective religion is true of any effective doctrine: It must be 'contrary to nature, to common sense and to pleasure.'"

—**Eric Hoffer**

"Sweep aside those hatred-eaten mystics, who pose as friends of humanity and preach that the highest virtue man can practice is to hold his own life as of no value."

—**Ayn Rand**

"The time has come for us brights to come out of the closet. What is a bright? A bright is a person with a naturalist as opposed to a supernaturalist world view. We brights don't believe in ghosts or elves or the Easter Bunny—or God. We disagree about many things, and hold a variety of views about morality, politics and the meaning of life, but we share a disbelief in black magic— and life after death. . . . Politicians don't think they even have to pay us lip service, and leaders who wouldn't be caught dead making religious or ethnic slurs don't hesi- tate to disparage the 'godless' among us."

—**Daniel C. Dennett**

Poets

Religion has indeed inspired poetry, but so has nonreligion. Poetry needs no purpose. It can simply be an observation, or a feeling, or an expression of beauty or pain, or a relishing of the sound of words. But it doesn't follow that those who write the poetry lack purpose in their lives. Many poets feel that writing about *this* world, the only real world, is much more beautiful and illuminating than writing about an imaginary world.

Philip Appleman

(1926–) | poet, Darwinian scholar

Not only is Appleman a distinguished poet, he is also a leading Darwin scholar. He edited the *Norton Critical Edition of Charles Darwin* as well as Malthus' *Essay on Population*. Appleman is one of those rare talents who blends science and art. He quips: "Today, like aardvarks, yaks, and gnus, / Prairie dogs are kept in zoos. / Surviving rodents, may we hope / You have a message for the pope?" I got to set some of Appleman's poems to music, including "In a Dark Time," which has these words: "Even as the preachers thunder Treason / And holy horrors dance with petty scandals / Even in this dusk, the dream of reason / Beckons with its flickering bright candles."

Robert Burns

(1759–1796) | poet, farmer

The "National poet of Scotland" clearly rejected Christianity and the afterlife, though it is uncertain whether he was an agnostic or a deist. "Auld Lang Syne" ("For Old Times' Sake"), sung by millions, marks the passing of the year not with religious sentiment but with human kindness. In a letter to a friend, Burns wrote: "These, my worthy friend, are my ideas. . . It becomes a man of sense to think for himself; particularly in a case where all men are equally interested, and where, indeed, all men are equally in the dark."

Samuel Taylor Coleridge

(1772–1834) | *poet*

Although Coleridge was probably a deist, he had kind words for atheists: "Not one man in ten thousand has goodness of heart or strength of mind to be an atheist." His views on religion were critical: "Whenever philosophy has taken into its plan religion, it has ended in skepticism; and whenever religion excludes philosophy, or the spirit of free inquiry, it leads to willful blindness and superstition."

John Keats

(1795–1821) | *poet, student*

Probably a deist, Keats rejected religion and refused religious ritual at his death at the age of 25, requesting only this line be engraved on his tombstone: "Here lies one whose name was writ in water." In his famous poem "Sonnet Written in Disgust of Vulgar Superstition," Keats describes the "melancholy" tolling of church bells as mourning the terminal illness of Christianity, which is "dying like an outburnt lamp."

Henry Wadsworth Longfellow

(1807–1882) | *poet, professor, abolitionist*

Longfellow's religious views were not constant. A friend wrote: "I think that as he grew older his hold upon anything like a creed weakened, though he remained of the Unitarian philosophy concerning Christ. He did not latterly go to church."

Percy Bysshe Shelley

(1792–1822) | *poet, student*

Shelley was expelled from Oxford University College for writing "The Necessity of Atheism," a pamphlet which opens with the words "There is no God." A passionate advocate of freethought, Shelly wrote: "If ignorance of nature gave birth to gods, knowledge of nature is made for their destruction."

Robert Louis Stevenson

(1850–1894) | *poet, novelist*

When poet and novelist rejected Christianity as a child, his Scots Presbyterian father called him an "'orrible atheist." One biographer wrote that Stevenson "was destitute of fixed creed or belief, and that he is properly described as an Agnostic." Not an outspoken atheist, Stevenson accommodated the religious beliefs of his family. His gravestone is inscribed with his secular poem, "Requiem":

> *Under the wide and starry sky*
> *Dig the grave and let me lie.*
> *Glad did I live and gladly die,*
> *And I laid me down with a will.*
> *This be the verse you 'grave for me:*
> *Here he lies where he long'd to be;*
> *Home is the sailor, home from the sea,*
> *And the hunter home from the hill.*

Algernon Charles Swinburne

(1837–1909) | *poet*

Swinburne launched his career with the collection *Atalanta in Calydon,* which refers to "the supreme evil,

God." In "Hertha," he wrote: ". . . the gods of your fashion . . . are worms that are bred in the bark that falls off; they shall die and not live." Joseph McCabe said of Swinburne that "No poet was ever less religious, or showed more plainly how little religion is needed for great artistic inspiration." In the poem, "Hymn of Man," Swinburne also wrote: "Glory to Man in the highest, for Man is the master of things."

More poets' quotes about religion

"Let us begin, then, at once, with that merest of words, 'Infinity.' This, like 'God,' 'spirit,' and some other expressions of which the equivalents exist in all languages, is by no means the expression of an idea—but of an effort at one. It stands for the possible attempt at an impossible conception."

—**Edgar Allan Poe**

"God is the only being who does not have to exist in order to reign."

—**Charles Baudelaire**

"When I was quite a boy, I had a spasm of religion which lasted six weeks . . . But I never since have swallowed the Christian fable."

—**George Meredith**

"The man who has no mind of his own lends it to the priests."

—**George Meredith**

"I know that a creed is the shell of a lie."

—**Amy Lowell**

"Goodbye, / Christ Jesus Lord God Jehovah, / Beat it on away from here now. / Make way for a new guy with no religion at all— / A real guy named / Marx Communist Lenin Peasant Stalin / worker ME . . ."
   —Langston Hughes

"So many Gods, so many creeds, / So many paths that wind and wind, / When just the art of being kind / Is all this sad world needs."
   —Ella Wheeler Wilcox

"I turned to speak to God / About the world's despair / But to make bad matters worse / I found God wasn't there."
   —Robert Frost

Political Leaders (U.S.)

Despite the importance in many times and places of maintaining at least a nominal religious affiliation as a prerequisite to electability, many of our great world leaders have been godless, or at least completely nonreligious.

Robert G. Ingersoll

(1833–1899) | politician, orator
Robert G. Ingersoll was a distinguished attorney, Civil War colonel, the first attorney general of Illinois, a friend of three U.S. presidents, and the most famous advocate of freethought in the United States in the 19th century. For 30 years he traveled the continent, speaking to

at-capacity crowds—50,000 came to hear him in Chicago and 40,000 had to be turned away. He spoke on Shakespeare, Burns, and Voltaire, but most listeners came to hear his critical lectures about the bible and religion. "All religions are inconsistent with mental freedom. Shakespeare is my bible, Burns my hymn-book," he wrote. To a reporter, he said, "With soap, baptism is a good thing." The words to Ingersoll's recitation, "Love," which has been performed at memorials and weddings, ends with the words: "With love, earth is heaven, and we are gods."

Ulysses S. Grant

(1822–1885) | military general, 18th U.S. President
Though raised in a Methodist family, Grant was not a member of any church and was never baptized. He was a friend of the irreverent Mark Twain and the famous agnostic orator Robert G. Ingersoll. Opposed to favoritism of religion, Grant warned of "the importance of correcting an evil that if permitted to continue, will probably lead to great trouble in our land . . . It is the acquisition of vast amounts of untaxed Church property . . . I would suggest the taxation of all property equally." As a student at West Point, when he received demerits for refusing to attend chapel, he protested that it is "not republican" to be forced to go to church. "Leave the matter of religion to the family altar, the Church, and the private schools, supported entirely by private contributions," Grant said in an 1875 speech. "Keep the church and state forever separate."

Culbert Olson

(1876–1962) | *California governor*

Although raised in a Utah Mormon family—his mother, a women's rights activist, became the state's first female elected official—Olson decided he was an atheist at the age of ten. Being sworn in as governor, he refused to say the entire oath of office. During his tenure, he resisted special tax breaks for the Catholic Church, a position that may have cost him his reelection. Joking to his successor, Earl Warren, he said: "If you want to know what hell is like, just be governor." Olson later became president of the United Secularists of America. "It is certain that organized religion and prayers to their almighty deity have not been the means of saving humanity from want or from wars, a large proportion of which have been wars for power between conflicting religious dogmas."

Robert Dale Owen

(1801–1877) | *U.S. Congressman*

A Scottish-Welsh immigrant, Owen came to the United States to help his father, social reformer Robert Owen, establish the utopian New Harmony commune in Indiana. Owen worked with Frances Wright on many reforms, including abolition, women's rights, pacifism, editing the *Free Enquirer*, and founding the Workingman Party. As a U.S. representative, he played a key role in founding the Smithsonian Institution and promoted public education. On September 17, 1862, Owen wrote President Lincoln urging him to use his power to end slavery. Owen did profess a belief in Spiritualism and wrote two popular books on the subject, though he admitted that his personal experience communicating with the dead had proven fraudulent. He was also the first author to advocate for birth control.

Jesse Ventura

(1951–) | Minnesota governor, former professional wrestler
A dark-horse candidate who was elected governor of Minnesota in 1998 on the Reform Party ticket, Ventura was known for provocative comments such as "Organized religion is a sham and a crutch for weak-minded people who need strength in numbers" (in a *Playboy* magazine interview). He backed gay rights, abortion rights, funding for higher education, third-party politics, mass transit, property tax reform, and opening trade relations with Cuba. He told the *Minnesota Independent*:

> *I believe in the separation of church and state. I was the only governor of all fifty who would not declare a National Day of Prayer. I took a lot of heat for that, and my response was very simple: Why do people need the government to tell them to pray? Pray all you want! Pray fifty times a day if you desire, it's not my business! . . . If I declare a National Day of Prayer, then I've got to declare a National No-Prayer Day for the atheists. They are American citizens too.*

Political Leaders (International)

Klas Pontus Arnoldson

(1844–1916) | *Nobel Laureate (Peace Prize)*

A member of the Swedish parliament from 1882 to 1887, Arnoldson promoted religious freedom, antimilitarism, and political neutrality for Sweden. His Nobel Peace Prize biography reports:

> *Familiar with the humanistic tenets of religious movements originating in the nineteenth century in Great Britain and in the New England section of the United States, he decried fanatic dogmatism and espoused essentially Unitarian views on truth, tolerance, freedom of the individual conscience, freedom of thought, and human perfectibility. These views he published in the Nordiska Dagbladet [Northern Daily] which he edited for a short time in the early 1870s, and in Sanningsskaren [The Truth Seeker].*

Michelle Bachelet

(1951–) | *President of Chile*

Bachelet made sure that her cabinet was half female and endured heavy criticism for her open agnosticism and secular reforms, infuriating the Catholic Church by making the morning-after pill free at state-run hospitals. "I'm agnostic," she told the *Washington Post*. "I believe in the state." In 2009, following her outstanding handling of the economic crisis, Bachelet's approval rating broke records at 80 percent. Explaining why she was such an unlikely candidate for a Roman Catholic country, Bachelet said: "I was a woman, a divorcee, a socialist, an agnostic . . . all possible sins together."

John Ballance

(1839–1893) | Prime Minister of New Zealand

Having witnessed frequent religious riots in his boyhood home of County Antrim, Ireland, Ballance rejected
religion and espoused a secularist philosophy. He was
described as a freethinker, "an outspoken Rationalist and
a high-minded Humanitarian." He and his wife emigrated
to New Zealand, where he became a jeweler, newspaper
publisher, and war hero. He was elected to parliament
and subsequently becape a cabinet minister under Prime
Minister Robert Stout. Later he became prime minister
himself and managed to pass progressive reforms, im-
proved government relations with Maoris, and called for
the "absolute equality of the sexes." Ballance secured the
right to vote for women in 1893, making New Zealand
the first nation to do so.

Charles Bradlaugh

*(1833–1891) | political activist, founder of the National
Secular Society*

England's best-known historical atheist, attorney Bradlaugh was elected to Parliament four times but was
refused seating because he would not take the religious
oath. He was finally seated in 1886 after a fight led by
loyal constituents. He persuaded Parliament to pass a
bill permitting the right of a secular affirmation in place
of a religious oath. "I maintain that thoughtful Atheism
affords greater possibility for human happiness than any
system yet based on, or possible to be founded on, The-
ism," Bradlaugh wrote, "and that the lives of true Atheists must be more virtuous—because more human—than

those of the believers in Deity . . . Atheism, properly
understood, is no mere disbelief; is in no wise a cold,
barren negative; it is, on the contrary, a hearty, fruitful
affirmation of all truth, and involves the positive asser-
tion of action of highest humanity."

Edvard Brandes
(1847–1931) | Danish politician, literary critic
A Danish writer and politician, Brandes edited several
radical political publications and wrote novels and plays
propounding rationalist and progressive ideals. When
elected to the Folketing in 1880, Brandes notably refused, as a freethinker, to take the religious oath. Despite
attempts to unseat him, he won the right to affirm. Even
with his openly atheist views, he was appointed to the
post of Minister of Finance.

Georges Clemenceau
(1841–1919) | Prime Minister of France
Though raised by Huguenot (French Protestant) family,
Clemenceau turned away from the faith while attending medical school and became an open opponent of the
school's religious emphasis. He became a mayor and
served five times in the National Assembly, then took a
temporary vacation from politics and became a journalist. His articles promoted rationalism and anticlericalism. Known as "the Tiger," he came back to politics and
was twice elected prime minister, a post he held through
the end of World War I. "Not only have the 'followers of
Christ' made it their rule to hack to bits all those who do
not accept their beliefs," Clemenceau wrote, "they have

also ferociously massacred each other, in the name of their common 'religion of love.'"

Robin Cook

(1946–2005) | Member of Parliament (U.K.)
Cook was Tony Blair's foreign affairs spokesman in 1994 and became Foreign Affairs Secretary in 1997. He quit his post in Blair's cabinet in 2003 because he had become "increasingly angry" about his failure to convince the prime minister to avoid war against Iraq. Cook died at the age of 59, and at his funeral, Reverend Richard Holloway told the mourners that as an avowed atheist Mr. Cook would have raised a "quizzical eyebrow" at the service being held in St. Giles Cathedral, but said it was an "entirely appropriate" venue because Mr. Cook was a 'Presbyterian atheist.'"

Giuseppe Garibaldi

(1807–1882) | revolutionary leader
Garibaldi spent most of his adult life as a leader of wars for independence. Exiled from his native Italy for advocating Italian, he fought alongside rebels in Brazil, Uruguay, and Prussia, finally returning to take part in the struggle for Italian independence. He went on to lead several attempts to capture Rome, then a sovereign state that was exempt from Italian unification, but was beaten back by the Papal Army. Inspired by him, followers ultimately seized all of Rome except the Vatican. Garibaldi was elected to the Italian Parliament in 1872 and is considered a national hero today. He called the Vatican "the Sacred Shop" and rejected all religious creeds. He wrote

in a letter: "Dear Friends, — Man has created God; not God man. — Yours ever, Garibaldi."

John Morley
(1838–1923) | *Member of Parliament (U.K.), writer, editor*
John Morley, who always spelled "God" with a small *g*, was a member of the English Parliament from 1883 to 1895. Editor of the rationalist *Fortnightly Review* and the crusading *Pall Mall Gazette*, he called for parliamentary reform and Irish home rule. Known as "honest John Morley," he was Chief Secretary for Ireland, Secretary of State for India, and Lord President of the Council. "Where it is a duty to worship the sun, it is pretty sure to be a crime to examine the laws of heat," Morley observed.

J. M. Robertson
(1856–1933) | *Member of Parliament (U.K.), journalist*
The Scottish-born Robertson was a member of the British Parliament from 1906 to 1918. He was also a rationalist, secularist, and freethought author who wrote for Charles Bradlaugh's National Reformer and became the paper's editor after Bradlaugh's death. He was a proponent of the "Jesus myth" theory, which asserted that Jesus was not a historical person, much less a god, but a fictional character created by the early church from past mythologies. His books critical of religion include *Christianity and Mythology* and *Pagan Christs*, which are still influential today, as well as *A Short History of Christianity* and *A Short History of Freethought Ancient and Mod-*

ern. "Petronius was surely right in saying Fear made the gods," Robertson wrote in *Pagan Christs*. "In primitive times fear of the unknown was normal; gratitude to an unknown was impossible."

Robert Stout
(1844–1930) | *Prime Minister of New Zealand*
Prime minister from 1884 to 1887, Stout was also president of the Dunedin Freethought Association. "We recognise no authority competent to dictate to us," he said. "Each must believe what he considers to be true and act up to his belief, granting the same right to everyone else." Stout promoted a secular educational system and as prime minister passed the Married Women's Property Act. He later served as Chief Justice and chancellor of New Zealand University. As a member of the Legislative Council, he defended secular education, which was being attacked by religious zealots attempting to introduce bible reading and prayers in school: "I fear that parliament may set up a little state church to make people morally good . . . it will make them immoral, for it will inaugurate bitterness and ill feeling."

Psychiatrists and Psychologists

Belief obviously has something to do with psychology. It makes sense that scientists who study the mind might be skeptical of the truth of the claims that arise from religious experiences.

Abraham H. Maslow

(1908–1970) | *psychologist, professor*

Best known for his "hierarchy of needs," Maslow recognized that "peak experiences" are not necessarily religious or supernatural. Biographer Richard J. Lowery describes Maslow's views in this manner: "We need not take refuge in supernatural gods to explain our saints and sages and heroes and statesmen, as if to explain our disbelief that mere unaided human beings could be that good or wise."

Carl Rogers

(1902–1987) | *psychologist*

One of the most eminent psychologists of the 20th century, Rogers was named Humanist of the Year by the American Humanist Association. His "self-directed" therapy was contrary to the established "tell me what to do" counseling at the time.

> *I disagree with manipulative approaches to therapy; to assume that one person can be in charge of another's life is a dangerous philosophy. My own philosophy is based on the conviction that people have within themselves the resources and capacity for self-understanding and self-correction. . . . In the [Northern Ireland encounter] groups, you see each other as a person, not as those evil Catholics and Protestants. The feelings of irrational hostility dissolve.*

B. F. Skinner

(1904–1990) | *psychologist, professor*

The founder of Behavioral Analysis recalled:

My Grandmother Skinner made sure that I understood
the concept of hell by showing me the glowing bed of coals
in the parlor stove. . . . Miss Graves [a teacher], though a
devout Christian, was liberal. She explained, for example,
that one might interpret the miracles in the Bible as figures
of speech. . . . Within a year I had gone to Miss Graves
to tell her that I no longer believed in God. "I know," she
said, "I have been through that myself." But her strategy
misfired: I never went through it.

Thomas Szasz

(1920–) | psychiatrist, professor

Szasz was named the 1973 Humanist of the Year by the American Humanist Association and was a Humanist Laureate with the Council for Secular Humanism. "If you talk to God, you are praying," Szasz observed. "If God talks to you, you have schizophrenia."

More psychiatrists' quotes about religion

"[Religion's] doctrines carry with them the stamp of the times in which they originated, the ignorant childhood days of the human race. Its consolations deserve no trust."
    —Sigmund Freud

"Religion is comparable to a childhood neurosis."
    —Sigmund Freud

"Ethical teaching is weakened if it is tied up with dogmas that will not bear examination."
    —Margaret Knight

Reformers and Revolutionaries

To be a reformer or revolutionary, needless to say, requires a certain disrespectful frame of mind. Its underlying mindset is, "We can do better than those authorities who have come before us." No wonder that many reformers have been nonbelievers or religious skeptics.

Felix Adler

(1851–1933) | *founder, Society for Ethical Culture*
Adler was raised Jewish but did not believe in a personal God. Explaining his new movement, which drew on influences as diverse as socialism, Judaism, and the works of Immanuel and Ralph Waldo Emerson, he said: "We propose entirely to exclude prayer and every form of ritual . . . to occupy that common ground where we may all meet, believers and unbelievers . . . be one with us where there is nothing to divide, in action. Diversity in creed, unanimity in the deed." His new society initiated social reforms such as a free kindergarten, free legal aid to the poor, and child labor laws. Adler was professor of social and political ethics at Columbia from 1902 until his death in 1933. "For more than three thousand years," he said,

> men have quarreled concerning the formulas of their faith. The earth has been drenched with blood shed in this cause, the face of day darkened with the blackness of the crimes perpetrated in its name. There have been no dirtier wars than religious wars, no bitterer hates than religious hates, no fiendish cruelty like religious cruelty; no baser baseness than religious baseness. It has destroyed the peace of fami-

lies, turned the father against the son, the brother against
the brother. And for what? Are we any nearer to unanim-
ity? On the contrary, diversity within the churches and
without has never been so widespread as at present. Sects
and factions are multiplying on every hand, and every
new schism is but the parent of a dozen others.

Mikhail Bakunin

(1814–1876) | Russian anarchist

This 19th-century Russian revolutionary participated in
the French and German revolutions of 1848. He was
twice arrested and sentenced to death, then extradited to
Russian prisons and exiled to Siberia before escaping and
settling in Geneva. In his 1872 work, *Statism and Anar-
chy*, he called for women's equality and free education.
"On behalf of human liberty, dignity and prosperity,"
Bakunin wrote, "we believe it our duty to recover from
heaven the goods which it has stolen and return them to
earth. . . . If God is, man is a slave; now, man can and
must be free; then, God does not exist." In *God and the
State*, he wrote, "If God really existed, it would be necessary to abolish Him."

Hypatia Bradlaugh Bonner

(1858–1943) | activist writer, editor

"Heresy makes for progress," was the motto of *Reformer*,
the British journal launched by the daughter of Charles
Bradlaugh, whose biography she wrote. Named after the
murdered pagan librarian of Alexandria, Hypatia was a
feminist, an opponent of the death penalty, an advocate
of penal reform, and a peace activist who lectured wide-

ly. "Away with all these gods and godlings," she wrote in her final article. "They are worse than useless."

Clarence Darrow

(1857–1938) | attorney

Clarence Darrow, the "Attorney for the Damned" who defended Eugene V. Debs and other labor activists, said, "I don't believe in God because I don't believe in Mother Goose." A passionate opponent of the death penalty, Darrow successfully argued to change the sentences of convicted killers Loeb and Leopold to life sentences. "Religion is the belief in future life and in God, he told the New York Times. "I don't believe in either." Darrow achieved international notoriety at the famous 1925 Scopes trial when he defended science teacher John Scopes, who was charged with teaching evolution in the public schools. "I do not consider it an insult, but rather a compliment to be called an agnostic. I do not pretend to know where many ignorant men are sure," he said during the trial.

Eugene V. Debs

(1855–1926) | union leader, Socialist Democratic presidential candidate (U.S.)

This labor organizer promoted women's and racial equality and justice for the poor, regularly blaming the church for retarding progress. "If I were hungry and friendless today, I would rather take my chances with a saloon-keeper than with the average preacher," he said. As a teenager, after listening to a fiery sermon, Debs said: "I left that church with rich and royal hatred of the priest as a person, and a loathing for the church as an institution, and I vowed that I would never go inside a church again." In 1893, Debs organized the first industrial union in the United States, the American Railway Union in Chicago. Debs and leaders of the union were arrested during the Pullman Boycott and Strike of 1894 and sent to jail for contempt of court. He ran for president five times as a candidate of the Socialist Democratic Party but never won a single electoral vote. Protesting World War I, he was convicted in federal court under the wartime espionage law, sentenced to ten years in prison, and disenfranchised for life. In prison, he was nominated to run for president and won nearly a million votes. Warren G. Harding commuted his sentence and released him in 1921. "The press and the pulpit have in every age and every nation been on the side of the exploiting class and the ruling class," Debs observed.

Emma Goldman

(1869–1940) | *anarchist*
"Since my earliest recollection of my youth in Russia I have rebelled against orthodoxy in every form," wrote Goldman. In the United States, arrested many times for her outspoken radical views, Goldman had to go into hiding in 1901 when a self-professed "anarchist" madman assassinated President William McKinley after claiming he had attended one of her lectures. At age 50, she was deported to the Soviet Union through the work of J. Edgar Hoover. Disillusioned with Bolshevism, she became a British citizen in 1925. "I do not believe in God, because I believe in man," Goldman wrote. "What-

ever his mistakes, man has for thousands of years been working to undo the botched job your god has made. There are . . . some potentates I would kill by any and all means at my disposal. They are Ignorance, Superstition, and Bigotry—the most sinister and tyrannical rulers on earth."

Joe Hill

(1879–1915) | *labor activist, songwriter*

Hill, a union organizer, itinerant laborer, poet, and song-writer, fought for the emancipation of the working class and women's right to vote. Falsely accused of murder in Utah, Helen Keller and President Woodrow Wilson tried to save his life, but in 1915, the beloved labor organizer was executed, his death making his cause for the union more widely known than it had been during his lifetime. According to the *Desert Evening News*, "No creed or religion found a place at the [funeral] service. There were no prayers and no hymns, but there was a mighty chorus of voices singing songs written by Hill." In his song, "The Preacher and the Slave," Joe Hill had observed: "Long-haired preachers come out every night, Try to tell you what's wrong and what's right: . . . 'You'll get pie in the sky when you die.' (That's a lie!)"

George Jacob Holyoake

(1817–1906) | *lecturer*

An ardent reformer who put causes over personal gain, Holyoake helped work for women's rights and political and educational reform and personally aided refugees fleeing persecution. He is best known for coining the term "secularist." Holyoake was sentenced to six months in jail for saying England was "too poor" to support a God, and should consider retiring him. He founded a number of freethought journals and wrote more than 160 pamphlets and works, including the book *Origin and Nature of Secularism* (1896), in which he wrote:

> *Free thought means fearless thought. It is not deterred by legal penalties, nor by spiritual consequences. Dissent from the Bible does not alarm the true investigator, who takes truth for authority not authority for truth. The thinker who is really free, is independent; he is under no dread; he yields to no menace; he is not dismayed by law, nor custom, nor pulpits, nor society—whose opinion appals so many. He who has the manly passion of free thought, has no fear of anything, save the fear of error.*

Rosa Luxemburg

(1871–1919) | Marxist theorist, founder of the Communist Party of Germany

A freethinking German revolutionary, Luxemburg was opposed to all forms of tyranny. Arrested for her views, beaten and thrown into a river, she continued to agitate for equality. No privileged level of society escaped her criticism: "The clergy, no less than the capitalist class, lives on the backs of the people, profits from the degradation, the ignorance and the oppression of the people," she wrote in 1905.

Karl Marx

(1818–1883) | *philosopher, economist, political theorist,*
originator of communism

Bertrand Russell once remarked that "[Karl Marx's] belief
that there is a cosmic force called Dialectical Materialism
which governs human history independently of human
volitions, is mere mythology." In fact, Marx never wrote
about this philosophy in his books, though an ongoing
correspondence with Joseph Dietzgen, who coined the
term, may have helped shape his rejection of religion in
his *Communist Manifesto*. A revolutionary who believed
that faith retards progress, Marx wrote: "Religion is the
sigh of the oppressed creature, the feelings of a heartless
world, just as it is the spirit of unspiritual conditions. It
is the opium of the people . . . The first requisite of the
happiness of the people is the abolition of religion."

Robert Owen

(1771–1858) | *factory owner, utopian leader, socialist advocate*
Owen, a Welsh immigrant, came to be known as known
as "a capitalist who became the first Socialist." Self-
educated, Owen was an unbeliever by 14. He put his
humanitarian creed into practice and established a model
community that attracted the attention of reformers
around the world. He set up the first infant-school in
Britain, a three-grade school for children under ten. He
sought to limit hours for child labor in mills, and saw
passage of the Factory Act in 1819. Clergy-led opposition rebuffed him when his views on religion became
widely known. Owen replied: "Relieve the human mind
from useless and superstitious restraints." His "Halls of

Science" attracted thousands of nonreligious followers, nicknamed "Owenites." After coming to America, he founded the New Harmony commune in Indiana. "Finding that no religion is based on facts and cannot therefore be true," he said during a debate, "I began to reflect what must be the condition of mankind trained from infancy to believe in errors."

Parker Pillsbury

(1809–1898) | *abolitionist, suffragist*

Parker Pillsbury was a Congregationalist minister but left the ministry over Christian complicity with slavery. The freethinking reformer and abolitionist activist edited The Herald of Freedom and The National Antislavery Standard. For 20 years, Pillsbury worked as an abolitionist agent and lecturer and became sympathetic to the cause of women, who had to fight to work on equal footing with male abolitionists. After the Civil War, Pillsbury collaborated with Elizabeth Cady Stanton as co-editor of The Revolution, published by Susan B. Anthony. His works include *Acts of the Anti-Slavery Apostles* (1883) and the critical *Church as It Is* (1884). He lectured widely on the "free religion" circuit in Ohio and Michigan, and was vice president of the New Hampshire Woman Suffrage Association. He wrote in a letter,

> *The Methodist Discipline provides for "separate Colored Conferences." The Episcopal church shuts out some of its own most worthy ministers from clerical recognition, on account of their color. Nearly all denominations of religionists have either a written or unwritten law to the same effect. In Boston, even, there are Evangelical churches whose pews*

are positively forbidden by corporate mandate from being
sold to any but "respectable white persons." Our incor-
porated cemeteries are often, if not always, deeded in the
same manner. Even our humblest village grave yards gener-
ally have either a "negro corner," or refuse colored corpses
altogether; and did our power extend to heaven or hell, we
should have complexional salvation and colored damnation.

Beatrice Webb

(1858–1943) | *reformer, health-care/education advocate*

Sydney Webb

(1859–1947) | *reformer, health-care/education advocate*

Beatrice (Potter) Webb, raised in privilege, devoted her
life to understanding and combating poverty. She was
one of the first to argue that poverty is not a deserved
condition but has real causes. Potter often disguised
herself as a poor worker and immersed herself in the
lifestyle of the poor. Working on a book project, she met
socialist reformer Sidney Webb. They married in 1892
and wrote many books together, including *The History
of Trade Unionism*. Personal friend H. G. Wells once
described the Webbs as "the most formidable and distinguished couple conceivable." They co-founded The London School of Economics and Political Science in 1895
to train social scientists to promote "the betterment of
society, and both held government posts throughout their
later years. Beatrice wrote: "That part of the Englishman's nature which has found gratification in religion is
now drifting into political life." Sidney Webb became a
Member of Parliament in 1892, the same year he married Beatrice. He and his wife were the first to devise a

national health plan, which was the origin of Britain's National Health Service. The Webbs' influence in British government is still felt in London politics today. In opposition to Britain's 1934 Poor Law, the Webbs wrote a minority report, which was considered a revolutionary document, responsible for the foundation of Britain's social services system. They were both freethinkers. "[False] generalizations [about socialism]," Sydney said, "are accordingly now to be met with only in leading articles, sermons, or the speeches of ministers or bishops."

Scientists

It is no surprise that religious belief in the scientific community is much lower than in the general population. Scientists, after all, are forced to respect evidence and reason, while religious claims are mainly based on faith. Since nature itself offers so much awe-inspiring wonder, there is no need to invent an imaginary god to worship.

Paul D. Boyer

(1918–) | biochemist
Boyer shared the Nobel Prize in Chemistry in 1997 with John E. Waller and Jens C. Skow "for their elucidation of the enzymatic mechanism underlying the synthesis of adenosine triphosphate (ATP)." A Deacon in the Mormon church, Boyer's views on religion were altered during graduate studies in science: "My views have changed from a belief that my prayers were heard to clear atheism . . . Over and over, expanding scientific knowledge has shown religious claims to be false. . . . None of the

beliefs in gods has any merit." In his short autobiography for the Nobel Peace Prize, Boyer wrote: "It is disappointing how little the understanding that science provides seems to have permeated into society as a whole. All too common attitudes and approaches seem to have progressed little since the days of Galileo. Religious fundamentalists successfully oppose the teaching of evolution, and by this decry the teaching of critical thinking. We humans have a remarkable ability to blind ourselves to unpleasant facts. This applies not only to mystical and religious beliefs, but also to long-term environmental consequences of our actions. If we fail to teach our children the skills they need to think clearly, they will march behind whatever guru wears the shiniest cloak. Our political processes and a host of human interactions are undermined because many have not learned how to gain a sound understanding of what they encounter."

Luther Burbank

(1849–1926) | *botanist*

The beloved botanist who developed more than 800 strains and varieties of plants, including the Shasta daisy and the Russet Burbank potato, did not believe in God. In a 1926 interview titled "I'm an Infidel, Declares Burbank, Casting Doubt on Soul Immortality Theory," Burbank said: ". . . as a scientist, I can not help feeling that all religions are on a tottering foundation. None is perfect or inspired. . . . The idea that a good God would send people to a burning hell is utterly damnable to me. I don't want to have anything to do with such a God."

John Burroughs

(1837–1921) | *naturalist, conservationist*

An essayist who popularized the American romantic view of nature, Burroughs wrote, "When I look up at the starry heavens at night and reflect upon what is it that I really see there, I am constrained to say, 'There is no God.'" In his 1910 journal, he wrote: "Joy in the universe, and keen curiosity about it all—that has been my religion."

Henry Cavendish

(1731–1810) | *physicist and chemist*

He discerned the composition of water and the atmosphere, took the first accurate measurement of the mass of the earth, and isolated hydrogen. Cavendish was secretive, reclusive, and asocial to the extreme. He did not attend church and was considered an agnostic. "As to Cavendish's religion, he was nothing at all," writes his biographer Dr. G. Wilson.

Francis Crick

(1916–2004) | *molecular biologist, physicist*

Crick wrote that as a child, "I was a skeptic, an agnostic, with a strong inclination toward atheism." Along with James Watson, and Maurice Wilkins, Crick won the Nobel Prize in Physiology or Medicine for the discovery of the structure and method of replication of the DNA molecule. "I realized early on," he wrote in his autobiography, "that it is detailed scientific knowledge which makes certain religious beliefs untenable. A knowledge of the true age of the earth and of the fossil record makes it impossible for any balanced intellect to believe in the

literal truth of every part of the Bible in the way that
fundamentalists do. And if some of the Bible is mani-
festly wrong, why should any of the rest of it be accepted
automatically? . . . What could be more foolish than
to base one's entire view of life on ideas that, however
plausible at the time, now appear to be quite erroneous?
And what would be more important than to find our
true place in the universe by removing one by one these
unfortunate vestiges of earlier beliefs?"

Marie Curie

(1837–1934) | *physicist, chemist*
Born to a devout Catholic mother and a staunchly atheistic father, the two-time Nobel Prize winner who coined
the word "radioactive" was a thoroughgoing rationalist.
"Pierre belonged to no religion and I did not practice
any," she wrote in her memoir of Pierre Curie.

Charles Darwin

(1809–1882) | *naturalist*
Though his father and uncle were freethinkers, Darwin
prepared to become an Anglican minister. A yearning to
travel pulled him away from his studies, and by the time
he returned from his first round-the-world sea voyage,
which lasted five years, he had discovered that his true
calling was natural history. "An agnostic would be the
most correct description of my state of mind," he wrote
to Rev. Fordyce. Darwin's monumental 1859 *Origin of
the Species* remains the framework by which all of biology makes sense. "I can indeed hardly see how anyone
ought to wish Christianity to be true," Darwin wrote in

his *Autobiography*, "for if so the plain language of the text seems to show that the men who do not believe, and this would include my Father, Brother, and almost all my best friends, will be everlastingly punished. And this is a damnable doctrine."

Richard Dawkins

(1941–) | evolutionary biologist, author
It is no secret that the prolific science writer affectionately known as "Darwin's pit bull" is an outspoken atheist. His book, *The God Delusion*, has become an international best seller. In his first popular book, *The Selfish Gene*, Dawkins proposed the concept of the cultural "meme" as another example (besides the gene) of a self-replicating naturally selected entity. His books *The Blind Watchmaker* and *Climbing Mount Improbable* directly counter creationist views. Dawkins wrote in 2001:

> *My respect for the Abrahamic religions went up in the smoke and choking dust of September 11th. The last vestige of respect for the taboo disappeared as I watched the Day of Prayer in Washington Cathedral, where people of mutually incompatible faiths united in homage to the very force that caused the problem in the first place: religion. It is time for people of intellect, as opposed to people of faith, to stand up and say "Enough!" Let our tribute to the dead be a new resolve: to respect people for what they individually think, rather than respect groups for what they were collectively brought up to believe.*

One of the bus signs put up by the Freedom From Religion Foundation contains this quote by Dawkins:

"The God of the Old Testament is arguably the most unpleasant character in all fiction."

Jean Baptiste Delambre

(1749–1822) | *astronomer, mathematician*

In his youth, the French astronomer briefly considered the priesthood but instead became a rationalist and tutored under the eminent atheist astronomer Joseph Lalande. Delambre recorded the transit of Mercury and calculated the orbit of Uranus, for which he won the Grand Prix by the Academy of Sciences. He went on to become the director of the Paris Observatory. He and Pierre Méchain made extensive measurements to the meridian of the earth, resulting in the standard length of the meter. "Conquests will come and go," Napoleon said, "but this work will endure."

Albert Einstein

(1879–1955) | *physicist, philosopher*

Raised in a nonpracticing Jewish family, Einstein sometimes used the word "God" metaphorically, as when he quipped, "God does not play dice with the universe," but he personally did not believe in God. In a letter to philosopher Eric Gutkind, Einstein wrote: "The word god is for me nothing more than the expression and product of human weaknesses, the Bible a collection of honorable, but still primitive legends which are nevertheless pretty childish. No interpretation no matter how subtle can (for me) change this." In a 1930 column for the *New York Times*, he said:

I cannot imagine a God who rewards and punishes the
objects of his creation, whose purposes are modeled after
our own—a God, in short, who is but a reflection of human
frailty. Neither can I believe that the individual survives
the death of his body, although feeble souls harbor such
thoughts through fear or ridiculous egotism. It is enough for
me to contemplate the mystery of conscious life perpetuat-
ing itself through all eternity, to reflect upon the marvelous
structure of the universe which we can dimly perceive, and
to try humbly to comprehend even an infinitesimal part of
the intelligence manifested in nature.

Einstein advised:

In their struggle for the ethical good, teachers of religion
must have the stature to give up the doctrine of a personal
God, that is, give up that source of fear and hope which
in the past placed such vast power in the hands of priests.
In their labors they will have to avail themselves of those
forces which are capable of cultivating the Good, the True,
and the Beautiful in humanity itself. This is, to be sure a
more difficult but an incomparably more worthy task.

Richard Feynman

(1918–1988) | quantum physicist
The legendary physicist won the 1965 Nobel Prize in
Physics for his work in quantum electrodynamics. When
Physics World polled scientists in 1999 asking them to
rank the greatest physicists, Feynman was rated seventh,
behind Galileo. An author and entertaining personality,
his first popular book was *Surely You're Joking, Mr. Feyn-*
man. Feynman described himself as "an avowed atheist"
in early youth. "I thought nature itself was so interesting

that I didn't want it distorted (by miracle stories). And so I gradually came to disbelieve the whole religion." He made headlines after being appointed to a commission investigating the 1986 *Challenger* shuttle disaster, when he demonstrated what went wrong with the O-rings. "Start out understanding religion by saying everything is possibly wrong. . . . As soon as you do that, you start sliding down an edge which is hard to recover from."

Stephen J. Gould

(1941–2002) | *paleontologist, author*

The theorist whose punctuated equilibrium transformed the Darwinian understanding of evolution, Gould proposed "non-overlapping magisteria"— a simple solution to the perceived conflict between science and religion in his book *Rock of Ages*. He wrote, "We are here because one odd group of fishes had a peculiar fin anatomy that could transform into legs for terrestrial creatures; because the earth never froze entirely during an ice age; because a small and tenuous species, arising in Africa a quarter of a million years ago, has managed, so far, to survive by hook and by crook. We may yearn for a 'higher answer'—but none exists."

Alan Hale

(1958–) | *physicist, astronomer*

The co-discoverer in 1995 of Comet Hale-Bopp wrote:

> *Oh, I have plenty of biases, all right. I'm quite biased toward depending upon what my senses and my intellect tell me about the world around me, and I'm quite biased against invoking mysterious mythical beings that other*

people want to claim exist but which they can offer no
evidence for. . . . By telling students that the beliefs of a
superstitious tribe thousands of years ago should be treated
on an equal basis with the evidence collected with our
most advanced equipment today is to completely under-
mine the entire process of scientific inquiry.

Edmund Halley

(1656–1742) | *astronomer*

The man who identified the famous comet that is named
after him was known as the "infidel mathematician." He
discovered many stars and clusters, encouraged Isaac
Newton to write his *Principia Mathematica*, invented the
diving bell, taught at Oxford, and became Royal Astronomer in 1720. Chalmers' *Biographical Dictionary* says:
"That he was an infidel in religious matters seems as
generally allowed as it appears unaccountable."

Frances Hamerstrom

(1908–1998) | *biologist, author*

Hamerstrom was the only woman to earn a graduate degree under Also Leopold, the only woman to share a nest
with a golden eagle, and the first woman to train and fly
a golden eagle. As parents, she and her husband had two
rules: "No chewing gum, and no church." Speaking of
her 55-year marriage to Frederick Hamerstrom (a nephew
of Charles Darwin), Fran quipped: "You'll notice that our
'pair bond' has lasted fairly well and I think it's because
we're both remarkably tolerant people. He's an agnostic
and I'm an atheist, and we've put up with each other
all this time!" During a speech to the Freedom From

Religion Foundation, Fran explained: "When I was eight years old, I tried prayer. And it didn't work!"

Stephen Hawking

(1942–) | *cosmologist*

Like Einstein, Hawking has sometimes used the word "God" metaphorically, but he has made it clear that he does not believe in a personal deity. In an ABC News interview, Hawking said: "There is a fundamental difference between religion, which is based on authority, [and] science, which is based on observation and reason. Science will win because it works." In his popular book *Black Holes and Baby Universes and Other Essays,* Hawking wrote: "All that my work has shown is that you don't have to say that the way the universe began was the personal whim of God."

Julian Huxley

(1887–1975) | *biologist*

The British scientist who expanded the evolutionary concept of natural selection said "[I am] not merely agnostic . . . I disbelieve in a personal God in any sense in which that phrase is ordinarily used. . . I disbelieve in the existence of Heaven or Hell in any conventional Christian sense." He promoted the concept of Religious Naturalism, holding that,

> *There is no separate supernatural realm: all phenomena are part of one natural process of evolution. There is no basic cleavage between science and religion. I believe that [a] drastic reorganization of our pattern of religious thought is now becoming necessary, from a god-centered to*

an evolutionary-centered pattern . . . Many people assert
that this abandonment of the god hypothesis means the
abandonment of all religion and all moral sanctions. This
is simply not true. But it does mean, once our relief at
jettisoning an outdated piece of ideological furniture is over,
that we must construct something to take its place.

An ant specialist, Huxley was Secretary of the Zoological Society of London and UNESCO's first general director from 1946 to 1948. "Operationally," Huxley wrote, "God is beginning to resemble not a ruler, but the last fading smile of a cosmic Cheshire Cat."

Thomas Huxley

(1825–1895) | physician, scientist
Nicknamed "Darwin's bulldog," Thomas Huxley is the person who coined the word "agnostic" (although Holyoake also claimed that honor). "In matters of the intellect," Huxley wrote, "follow your reason as far as it will take you, without any other consideration. And negatively, in matters of the intellect do not pretend that conclusions are certain which are not demonstrated or demonstrable." Huxley was president of the Royal Society. He was elected to the London School Board in 1870, where he promoted commonsense reforms. "Skepticism is the highest duty," he wrote, "and blind faith the one unpardonable sin."

Donald C. Johanson

(1943–) | paleoanthropologist
Johanson is the paleoanthropologist who discovered "Lucy," the Ethiopian australopithecus fossil that is a direct ancestor of humans. During an interview on

Freethought Radio, Johanson said: "Religion is a way of making up a myth to explain why we're here. . . I'm an atheist, and am very comfortable with that. I've never felt the need to believe in some creator-being for this happening." When Annie Laurie Gaylor asked about the importance of Lucy, he said:

> *The real significance of Lucy is that not only is she a link to our past, but more importantly a link to the natural world. When people who are very religious disregard the natural world around them, I think that is the 'biggest sin' we could ever commit. We have the creator. We know the creator. The creator is the natural world. . . . We're all connected by DNA. Every living organism has the same building blocks. The process of evolution by means of natural selection is the creator of all diversity on this planet. Lucy . . . reconnects us to our roots, and our roots are based in the natural world. It is really incumbent on all of us to protect that natural world, to look after that natural world, not to disregard it and destroy it, cut it down, and pollute it, and so on. We wouldn't want to do that, if we were a religious person, to our "Creator," yet the very creator who created us is the natural world, and we are miserably unkind to her.*

Harold Walter Kroto

(1939–) | chemist

The British scientist became one of three co-recipients of the Nobel Prize in Chemistry for co-discovering a new molecule, the C60 species, while examining the atmosphere of a carbon star. A musician, sports enthusiast, and artist, Kroto wrote in his Nobel Prize autobiography:

*The desperate need we have for such organisations as
Amnesty International has become, for me, one of the
pieces of incontrovertible evidence that no divine (mystical)
creator (other than the simple Laws of Nature) exists. . . .
The illogical excuses, involving concepts such as free will(!),
convoluted into confusing arguments by clerics and other
self-appointed guardians of universal morality, have always
seemed to me to be just so much fancy (or actually clumsy)
footwork devised to explain why the fascinating and beauti-
fully elegant world I live in operates exactly the way one
would expect it to in the absence of a mystical power.*

Fridtjof Nansen

(1861–1930) | explorer

A championship cross-country skier and ice skater, Nan-
sen won public acclaim by leading the first expedition
across Greenland. Later, he won the Nobel Peace Prize
in 1922 for arranging the swap of 400,000 prisoners
of war and worked with the League of Nations and the
International Red Cross. "The religion of one age is, as a
rule, the literary entertainment of the next," he said during a speech.

Linus Pauling

(1901–1994) | scientist, peace activist, humanitarian

Considered the founding father of molecular biology,
Dr. Pauling was the only person to receive two unshared
Nobel Prizes: for Chemistry in 1954 and Peace in 1962.
Raised as a Lutheran, he attended the Unitarian Univer-
salist Church throughout his adult life but declared two
years before his death that he was actually an atheist.
"The only sane policy for the world is that of abolishing

war," he said during his Peace Prize acceptance speech. He was an unorthodox Unitarian for many years. "It is sometimes said that science has nothing to do with morality," he wrote. "This is wrong. Science is the search for truth, the effort to understand the world; it involves the rejection of bias, of dogma, of revelation, but not the rejection of morality."

Oliver Sacks

(1933–) | *neurologist, psychologist*

The neurologist and popular science author describes himself as "an old Jewish atheist" in his autobiography, *Uncle Tungsten*. The Oscar-nominated film *Awakenings*, in which Sacks is played by actor Robin Williams, was based on his book by the same name. Accepting the Emperor Has No Clothes Award in 2005 from the Freedom From Religion Foundation (of which he is an Honorary Board Member), Sacks said:

> *I am horrified to think that 70 percent of the U.S. population, so it is said, believes in angels, aliens, spirits, spooks of one sort or another. Sometimes I think what Freud called "the black mud of occultism" is sweeping this country. When one is too excited by the idea of things supernatural, one may not pay enough attention to the natural. One cannot see how wonderful nature is if one is too concerned with super-nature. For me, and for all of us sympathetic to the spirit of Spinoza, nature is infinitely more wonderful than any religious concept. And it does not demand an abrogation of one's reason.*

Carl Sagan

(1934–1996) | astronomer, author

The director of the Laboratory for Planetary Studies at Cornell and co-founder of the Planetary Society produced the award-winning PBS series *Cosmos*, which was watched by 500 million people in 60 countries. With his wife, Ann Druyan, he co-produced the popular movie *Contact*, which featured a feminist, atheist protagonist. "If some good evidence for life after death were announced," Sagan wrote, "I'd be eager to examine it; but it would have to be real scientific data, not mere anecdote. As with the face on Mars and alien abductions, better the hard truth, I say, than the comforting fantasy. And in the final tolling it often turns out that the facts are more comforting than the fantasy." In the epilogue to Sagan's last book, *Billions and Billions: Thoughts on Life and Death at the Brink of the Millennium*, published posthumously in 1997, Ann Druyan gives a moving account of Carl's last days:

> *Contrary to the fantasies of the fundamentalists, there was no deathbed conversion, no last minute refuge taken in a comforting vision of a heaven or an afterlife. For Carl, what mattered most was what was true, not merely what would make us feel better. Even at this moment when anyone would be forgiven for turning away from the reality of our situation, Carl was unflinching. As we looked deeply into each other's eyes, it was with a shared conviction that our wondrous life together was ending forever.*

Robert Sapolsky

(1957–) | neurologist, author

Sapolsky has dedicated his life to studying primates and stress. His book, *The Primate's Memoir*, recounts his adventures during years of living with baboons in Africa. "There's a remarkable parallelism between religious ritualism and the ritualism of OCD," he said during a speech to the Freedom From Religion Foundation. "In OCD, the most common rituals are the rituals of self-cleansing, of food preparation, of entering and leaving holy places of emotional significance, and rituals of numerology. You look in every major religion, and those are the four most common ritual forms that you see. You could say it's just by chance; or you could say here's a biological convergence going on there." Sapolsky does not bemoan the lack of religion in his life: "The purpose of science in understanding who we are as humans is not to rob us of our sense of mystery, not to cure us of our sense of mystery. The purpose of science is to constantly reinvent and reinvigorate that mystery. To always use it in a context where we are helping people in trying to resist the forces of ideology."

Ellery Schempp

(1940–) | physicist

One of the scientists who worked on the development of fiber optics and the MRI system, Schempp was also the plaintiff in the landmark 1963 Supreme Court *Abington School District v. Schempp* decision, which removed the recitation of the bible and the Lord's Prayer from public schools. "Public prayer," he argued, "is not intended to

183

promote religious values, but to enhance the authority of some churches and some political views over others. Similarly with the posting of the Ten Commandments. It is about power, not about religion. Government by Christian or Islamic or any other faith has rarely been progressive. . . . And the Constitution clearly intends that there should be freedom from religion."

William Smith

(1769–1839) | geologist

The English surveyor who produced the world's first geological map in 1815 is known as the "Father of Geology." Biographer Simon Winchester, reporting that Smith's "agnosticism was well-known," writes that "For the first time the earth had a provable history, a written record that paid no heed or obeisance to religious teaching and dogma, that declared its independence from the kind of faith that is no more than the blind acceptance of absurdity. A science . . . had now at last broken free from the age-old constraints of doctrine and canonical instruction."

Victor Stenger

(1935–) | physicist

A pioneer in neutrino astronomy, Stenger wrote,

> *The message of New Atheism has been terribly misunderstood as being exclusively negative. For every negative we have an even greater positive. Faith is absurd and dangerous and we look forward to the day, no matter how distant, when the human race finally abandons it. Reason is a noble substitute, proven by its success. Religion is an intellectual and moral sickness that cannot endure forever*

if we believe at all in human progress. Science sees no limit in the human capacity to comprehend the universe and ourselves. God does not exist. Life without God means we are the governors of our own destinies.

James D. Watson

(1928–) | molecular biologist

A co-discoverer of the double helix structure of DNA, Watson said, "The biggest advantage to believing in God is you don't have to understand anything, no physics, no biology. I wanted to understand." As a young man, he "came to the conclusion that the church was just a bunch of fascists that supported Franco. I stopped going on Sunday mornings and watched the birds with my father instead." Watson's popular book, *The Double Helix*, has become a best seller. "Every time you understand something," he said in an interview, "religion becomes less likely. Only with the discovery of the double helix and the ensuing genetic revolution have we had grounds for thinking that the powers held traditionally to be the exclusive property of the gods might one day be ours."

Stephen Weinberg

(1933–) | physicist

Weinberg, who won the 1979 Nobel Prize in Physics for co-discovering the electro-weak force, is an atheist who does not think science and religion can be reconciled. "With or without religion," he said, "good people can behave well and bad people can do evil; but for good people to do evil—that takes religion."

More scientists' quotes about religion

"I cannot believe in the immortality of the soul. . . . I am an aggregate of cells, as, for instance, New York City is an aggregate of individuals. Will New York City go to heaven? . . . No; nature made us—nature did it all—not the gods of the religions."
—**Thomas A. Edison**

Songwriters

Irving Berlin

(1888–1989) | songwriter—best known: "God Bless America," "White Christmas," "Alexander's Ragtime Band," "Easter Parade"

Irving Berlin was by any measure the greatest composer of popular American music, with hundreds of enduring hits. Born into a Russian Jewish family that came to New York City when he was five years old to escape religious persecution, Berlin quickly shed his religious roots and fell in love with America. "Patriotism was Irving Berlin's true religion," writes biographer Laurence Bergreen.

"Though he is not a religious person," his daughter Mary Ellin Barrett recalls, "doesn't even keep up appearances of being an observant Jew, he does not forget who his people are." Irving and his nominally Catholic wife, Ellin, were married in an unannounced secular ceremony at the Municipal Building, not a church or synagogue. They had three daughters. "Both our parents," Mary Ellin recalls, "would pass down to their children the moral and ethical values common to all great religions; give us a sense of what was right and what was wrong; raise us not to be good Jews or good Catholics or good whatever else you might care to cite, but to be (or try to be) good human beings . . . [W]hen we grew up . . . all three of us would share our father's agnosticism and sidestep our husbands' faiths."

The man who wrote "White Christmas" actually hated Christmas. He needed a melody for a 1942 movie called *Holiday Inn,* which called for a song for each American holiday. "White Christmas" is not religious. It is not about the birth of a savior-god. It is about winter, the real reason for the season.

Just as "White Christmas" is not about Christ, "God Bless America" is not about God. It is about love for America. " 'God Bless America' revealed that patriotism was Irving Berlin's true religion," Bergreen writes. "It evoked the same emotional response in him that conventional religious belief summoned in others; it was his rock." His choice of "God bless" was simply picking up an American idiom that the characters in his musical might say, not expressing his own personal belief. "God Bless America" was originally written in 1918 for *Yip, Yip, Yaphank,* a World War I show about the U.S. Army. As he was finishing the musical, he added a patriotic melody that he imagined the soldier characters would sing. But Berlin was not satisfied with the song, and it lay on a shelf forgotten for two decades. In 1938, Kate Smith was looking for a "song of peace" for her Armistice Day broadcast. Irving Berlin tried writing a couple of songs for her, but they were "too much like making a speech to music," he said. It then occurred to him to dig up that discarded tune from 1918.

Irving Berlin sometimes poked fun at faith. In 1922, confronting censors, he wrote "Pack Up Your Sins and Go to the Devil in Hades" for his *Music Box Revue*. The lyrics went in part, "They've got a couple of old reformers in heaven, making them go to bed at eleven. Pack up your sins and go to the devil, and you'll never have to go to bed at all." Berlin died quietly at home at the age of 101. He did not believe in an afterlife, but maybe he did jokingly wish for a hell, because "all the nice people are there," as his lyrics tell us.

Stephen Foster

(1826–1864) | songwriter—best known: "Oh, Susanna," "Camptown Races," "Old Folks at Home," "My Old Kentucky Home"

Stephen Foster, who was appropriately born on the Fourth of July, wrote the first great American popular songs. He was the first American songwriter to support himself from music sales, propelling the industry in its infancy. He produced a body of songs that have been remembered and sung longer than the works of any other American songwriter. Irving Berlin honored Foster by quoting part of the "Swanee River" in his first hit, "Alexander's Ragtime Band" (he had a picture of Foster on his office wall). George Gershwin paid him a similar tribute with his first hit song, "Swanee." They knew that if you wanted to tap into the culture of America, you had to start with Stephen Foster.

Little is known of Stephen Foster's inner religious
views, but he lived and worked as if he were not a believer. A nonconformist, he never joined a church and
rarely attended services. None of his music can be said
to be inspired by religious faith. The songs that he chose
to write of his own volition were purely secular.

Toward the end of his life, he accepted an assign-
ment writing Sunday School songs. "He hadn't found
God, but he had found a publisher," his biographer
writes. The songs were part of an endeavor to indoctri-
nate children with "catchy" music, sometimes setting
religious words to secular melodies. Perhaps the original
lyrics to "Some Folks" (1855) give us a glimpse into
Stephen Foster's own views, a liberal attitude of live-and-
let-live as well as his celebration of "life before death."
Some of the words appear to be a rebuke to Puritanism:

> *Some folks like to sigh,*
> *Some folks do; Some folks do.*
> *Some folks long to die,*
> *But that's not me nor you.*
> *Some folks fret and scold,*
> *Some folks do; Some folks do;*
> *They'll soon be dead and cold,*
> *But that's not me nor you.*
> *Long live the merry, merry heart*
> *That laughs by night and day,*
> *Like the Queen of Mirth,*
> *No matter what some folks say.*

The lyrics for his 1846 utopian song, "There's a
Good Time Coming," do not point to an afterlife or the-

ocracy. They yearn rather for a time of tolerance, when religious divisiveness shall be eliminated:

> *Shameful rivalries of creed*
> *Shall not make the martyr bleed,*
> *In the good time coming.*
> *Religion shall be shorn of pride,*
> *And flourish all the stronger;*
> *And Charity shall trim her lamp;*
> *Wait a little longer.*

Stephen Foster may not have been an atheist—it is hard to know—but he certainly lived like a nonbeliever and wrote as a humanist, inspired by a hope for *this* world.

Ira Gershwin

(1896–1983) | *lyricist—best known:* Porgy and Bess

George Gershwin

(1898–1937) | *composer—best known:* Rhapsody in Blue, An American in Paris

Biographer Deena Rosenberg writes,

> *For a family of Eastern European Jewish immigrants, the Gershwins led a relatively secularized existence. At home they spoke only English, not Russian or Yiddish. Of the three sons, only Ira (who was born Isidore) had a bar mitzvah, and as he recalled it later, the ceremony did not mean much to him. . . . The Gershwins' Judaism was neither religious nor politicized. It was cultural and casual—and as such, it was a Judaism from which George and Ira never felt estranged.*

Biographer Rodney Greenberg records that

The two brothers roamed all over New York City in their
youth, absorbing the culture of Chinatown, Harlem and
the West Side just as much as Italian, Irish and Jewish
sources. They were not imbued with Jewish ritual and
practice in their boyhood, when it would have had most
effect. Rose [mother] made sure the living-room curtains
were drawn closed on the eve of sabbaths or festivals, so
that her Jewish neighbours would be unaware she had not
lit the ceremonial candles. Ira did seem to retain a fond-
ness for one religious ceremony: the annual Passover seder
meal . . . but we know from the harmonica virtuoso Larry
Adler that, on the evening he was invited to Ira's house to
celebrate the festival, Ira wore a silly top-hat like a vaude-
ville comedian, and had rewritten the ancient text for
maximum comic effect.

The lyrics to "It Ain't Necessarily So" (the title was
suggested by George) are decidedly irreverent, taking the
gospel "with a grain of salt." The song has become something of a freethought anthem among nonbelievers: "The
things that yo' li'ble to read in the Bible, it ain't necessarily so." An unpublished verse was held for encores:

'Way back in 5,000 B.C.
Ole Adam an' Eve had to flee.
Sure, dey did dat deed in
De Garden of Eden–
But why chasterize you and me?

Only a freethinker could write such irreverent words.
Regarding inspiration, George had this to say:
"When we most want it, it does not come. Therefore the
composer does not sit around and wait for an inspiration

to walk up and introduce itself. What he substitutes for it is nothing more than talent plus his knowledge."

George Gershwin had major plans for musicals and dreams of serious concert works when his life was tragically cut short at age 39 by an undiagnosed brain tumor. (If it had been diagnosed, he still could not have been saved, even with today's medicine.) Before he lapsed into a coma, he was thinking and talking about his future work, all ambitious projects. After George died, Ira continued to work and write songs for 46 more years.

Jay Gorney

(1896–1990) | composer—best known: "Brother, Can You Spare a Dime?" and "You're My Thrill"
The composer of "Brother, Can You Spare a Dime?" was, like the lyricist Yip Harburg, a nonbeliever who ended up being blacklisted for his liberal views. Jay Gorney is the man who discovered Shirley Temple and for whom he wrote her first movie song "Baby, Take a Bow." He wrote many "standards" and hundreds of popular songs for theater, film, and television.

"We were not a religious family," his widow Sondra Gorney told me in a telephone interview. They were not married in a church or synagogue. His memorial was held at the New York Public Shakespeare Theater, not in a religious setting. The son of Polish-Jewish immigrants who came to the United States escaping religious persecution when he was a child, Jay Gorney became more involved with liberal human causes than with any religious heritage. "Jay's entire life was dedicated to helping his fellow man and woman, as an artist and as a concerned human being," Sondra tells us. Music, for Gorney, was more than entertainment—it was a way to make *this* world a better place.

Yip Harburg

(1896–1981) | *lyricist—best known: "Over the Rainbow," "Brother, Can You Spare a Dime," "April in Paris"*
According to the American Film Institute's list of Top 100 Movie Songs, "Over the Rainbow" is number one. It is the one song that "everybody knows." The music was written by Harold Arlen and the words by Yip Harburg. It won the 1939 Oscar for Best Original Song.

Yip Harburg was born in New York's Lower East Side to immigrant Russian Jewish parents. In school, he sat alphabetically in the desk next to his childhood friend and future lyricist Ira Gershwin, another nonbeliever who was to change the face of popular American music. Although he was raised Jewish, music very quickly replaced religion for Yip Harburg. He explains part of the reason:

> My parents were Orthodox Jews, though not as strict as the Hassidim. To some extent, they were tongue-in-cheek Orthodox. My father did go to shul regularly and I usually went with him. Whatever religious feeling I had evaporated when I was about 15 in the face of a devastating personal crisis. I had an elder brother, Max, twelve years my senior—my hero—my inspiration. . . . Max became a famous scientist. . . . And then, at age 28, he died of cancer. My mother, broken by the shock, died [some years] after. The tragedy left me an agnostic. I threw over my religion. I began seeing the world in a whole new light. . . . The

House of God never had much appeal for me . . . Anyhow,
I found a substitute temple—the theater.

Yip Harburg started an appliance business, but when
it went bankrupt after the Great Crash of 1929, leaving
him deep in debt, he happily turned to songwriting, his
true love. When Arthur Freed at MGM was looking for
music for *The Wizard of Oz,* he jumped at the chance to
work with Harburg. Although Freed was a "flag waver of
the first order," and could not comprehend Yip's social
imperative, he admired and respected his genius and
whimsy with words. Freed handed control of the book
and songs to Harburg, who made the movie a brilliant
success, rewriting whole scenes, replacing entire stretch-
es of dialogue with song. Much of the movie—including
the scene where the Wizard hands out medals—was written by Yip, though he is credited only as "lyricist." The
film was a moderate success in its time, mainly because
at the time it was the most expensive movie ever made,
but after yearly broadcasts on television since the 1950s,
"Over the Rainbow" has become a global treasure.

The wildly successful *Finian's Rainbow,* produced in
1947, was conceived by Harburg as a socialist attack on
capitalism and racial inequality. The show had a smash
run of 725 performances on Broadway, introducing hits
such as "Old Devil Moon," "How Are Things in Glocca
Morra?" and "Look to the Rainbow." Musical librettist
Peter Stone wrote: *"Finian's Rainbow* was . . . extraordi-
narily political, [but] the audience had no idea of that. .
. . If you ever want to reach people with a political tract,
go study *Finian's Rainbow."* When Harburg's name hit
the Hollywood blacklist in 1950, he was shocked. "I am

outraged by the suggestion that somehow I am connected with, believe in, or am sympathetic with Communist or totalitarian philosophy." Nonetheless, he was effectively barred from Hollywood for a decade.

Harburg also wrote light satiric verses poking holes in all things sacred, with titles like "Atheist," "Do Unto Others?" and "How Odd of God." These poems, including some newly discovered verses, have been republished in the book *Rhymes for the Irreverent*.

Harburg's children, Ernie and Marge, grew up to share their father's freethinking views. Ernie, a retired research scientist, told me a story about his dad's world view. Yip and his cousin Herman Meltzer were riding in a bouncing plane in bad weather when the pilot announced they were having trouble, asking the passengers to prepare for a possible crash landing. Fearing the worst, Herman asked Yip, "Do you believe in God?" Yip thought for a moment and then said, "I'll tell you when we land."

Still working, nearing his 85th birthday, Yip Harburg died in 1981 due to a massive heart convulsion while driving to a story conference for a film version of *Treasure Island*. In one of his poems (recently rediscovered), he had observed:

They who live on love and laughter
Don't mess around with the hereafter.

Yip Harburg did not believe in an afterlife "over the rainbow." He was inspired by beauty, hope, and humanity. He knew there is a place in the human heart where "dreams really do come true," and hoped that our future would be free of fanaticism and violence.

Scott Joplin

(1868–1917) | pianist, ragtime composer—best known: "Maple Leaf Rag"

Although the history is thin, and the personal views of the King of Ragtime are hard to determine, we can be quite certain that Scott Joplin was not religious. Joplin's early musical career took place in centers of entertainment, not in church. He played piano in a brothel and in a club that was shut down due to pressure from local churches, whose pastors were ashamed of the "iniquitous practices" (dancing) taking place there.

Ragtime was America's first uniquely national style of music. Scott Joplin, born in Texas and raised in Missouri, did not invent ragtime, but it was his incredible compositions that propelled it to national prominence.

Joplin never wrote religious music. He was married in a home, not a church, nor was his funeral conducted in a church.

A glimpse into Joplin's personal views might be found in the words of the one opera he wrote, *Treemonisha*, which was never completely performed during his lifetime. "The subject," writes biographer Edward A. Berlin, "is really the African-American community which, as seen by Joplin fewer than fifty years after emancipation, was still living in ignorance, superstition, and misery. The way out of this condition, he tells his intended audience, is with the education that can be provided by white society." He does not propose religion as the solution. "Ignorance is criminal," he tells his audience. Even the religious characters in the musical refer to the "Creator," not the "Lord God" or the "Jesus" of spirituals and hymns.

Why should Joplin have rejected the church? Berlin wonders. "Because the churches rejected what was important to him—ragtime, dance, and the theater." Whatever Joplin's private views may have been, it is clear that his music was not inspired by religion. "There is no harm in musical sounds," Joplin said, reflecting the view of many composers that music simply speaks for itself. "It matters not whether it is fast ragtime or a slow melody like 'The Rosary,'" he continued, implying that there is no such thing as religious music, or nonreligious music. Music is just music.

Jerome Kern

(1885–1945) | songwriter—best known: Show Boat

Jerome Kern is most responsible for making the Broadway musical different from anything that had come before, breaking entirely from European traditions, creating a style of singable melody that has come to be known as "American," the fount from which 20th-century songwriters drank. The 1927 musical *Show Boat* (lyrics by Oscar Hammerstein) was ground-breaking in its integration of music and story. Songs such as "Ol' Man River" (Kern's favorite) and "Can't Help Lovin' That Man," as well as "The Way You Look Tonight" (1936 Academy Award, lyrics by Dorothy Fields), "Smoke Gets In Your Eyes," "All the Things You Are," "The Last Time I Saw Paris" (1941 Academy Award, lyrics by Oscar Hammerstein), "A Fine Romance," "Long Ago (And Far Away)," and dozens more Kern melodies have defined what it means to be a "standard."

This "inspired" songwriter, the "Father of American Music," as many referred to him, did not believe in God. Jerome Kern's parents were German-Jewish immigrants who had no use for religion. "Their marriage at Temple Emanu-El was the last religious function in either of their lives," writes biographer Michael Freedland. They gave their son no religious training, and "the Jewish faith, of which he never consciously felt himself a member" was simply social custom. "I don't let a single day pass without writing something," he once said, explaining why he worked on the Sabbath and on holidays. "His religion was his music and his lifestyle—his enjoyment of elegance and his voracious appetite for having a good time," Freedland writes. He didn't need religion to have a full and ethical life.

Burton Lane

(1912–1997) | *composer—best known:* Finian's Rainbow, Singin' in the Rain, Babes on Broadway
Burton Lane's most popular work was the score for the hit Broadway musical *Finian's Rainbow*, on which he collaborated with the witty and irreverent lyricist Yip Harburg. Born in New York City, Lane studied classical piano as a child. He became one of the rare composers able to work successfully on Broadway as well as in Hollywood, writing musicals and composing music for more than 30 movies. He had his first song published when he was 15. At age 17, he met the Gershwins and was introduced into the society of first-rank songwriters, including Yip Harburg. Lane discovered young singer Frances Gumm, who changed her name to Judy Garland.

There is no proper biography of Burton Lane, but Annie Laurie Gaylor and I were able to interview his widow,
Lynn Lane, on Freethought Radio during the revival of
Finian's Rainbow on Broadway in 2009–2010. I asked
Ms. Lane how her nonbelieving husband got along with
Yip Harburg, who was known for his agnostic and progressive views. "They were exactly on the same wave-
length," she told us. "Yip was writing the words, so more
of what he felt was evident in his work. When you're
writing the music, there are no lyrics, so what you get,
you get from the melody, and that does not show your
political opinions. I don't think there was anything of any
real consequence that Burton and Yip disagreed about."

One of the funnest songs from *Finian's Rainbow* is
"The Begats," including these irreverent lyrics:

The Lord made Adam. The Lord made Eve.
He made them both a little bit naive.
They lived as free as the summer breeze,
Without pajamas and without chemise,
Until they stumbled on the apple tree.

Then she looked at him, and he looked at her,
And they knew immediately what the world was fer.
He said, "Give me my cane." He said, "Give me my hat.
The time has come to begin the begat."

So they begat Cain, and they begat Abel,
Who begat the rabble at the Tower of Babel.
They begat the Cohens, and they begat O'Rourkes.
And they begat the people who believe in storks . . .

Burton Lane, who didn't mind mocking religion,
came up with a creative melody that matches the genius
of Yip's whimsical, freethought lyrics.

199

Cole Porter

(1891–1964) | songwriter—best known: "Anything Goes,"
"I Love Paris," "I've Got You Under My Skin," "My Heart
Belongs to Daddy," "De-Lovely," "Night and Day," Can-Can

Cole Porter, composer of hundreds of American show
tunes and standards (he wrote both words and music),
was born into a nominally Protestant family. His father
was "a good man but not burdened by religion," writes
biographer William McBrien. His mother went to church
as a matter of social habit. Porter, McBrien writes, "was
never a believer, and his several comments about his
mother's attachments to Peru [Indiana] churches were
dismissive . . . Cole developed no deeply felt religious
beliefs. On most occasions throughout his life, he spoke
of 'pleasing the gods' or lamented, 'The gods are punish-
ing me,' but he seldom referred to God, except to deny
belief in Him."

Porter and his wife, Linda, had a lifelong, loving
(though sexless) marriage, in which his homosexuality
and lifestyle were acknowledged and encouraged. Believers and nonbelievers, gays and non-gays, all of us have
been enriched by the songs that this nonconformist gave
us. When Cole Porter was admitted to the hospital for
the last time, a nurse who was filling out the admittance
form asked Porter about religious affiliations:

"Put down none," Cole replied.

"Protestant?"

"Put down—none."

Richard Rodgers

(1902–1979) | *composer—best known:* Oklahoma!, Carousel, South Pacific, The King and I, The Sound of Music

Richard Rodgers, one of the great composers of musical theater, was an atheist. He was born on Long Island, New York, to a prosperous Jewish family with an atheist grandmother. While attending Columbia University, he met his first major songwriting partner, lyricist Lorenz Hart, then studied serious music at the Institute of Musical Art, known today as Juilliard.

Rodgers and Hart became a huge songwriting force on Broadway. During the 1920s and 1930s they produced the hit musicals *Babes in Arms, Pal Joey,* and *The Boys from Syracuse.* After Hart's early death, Rodgers teamed up with Oscar Hammerstein II, also nonreligious, to produce *Oklahoma!* (1943) and ten more musicals. After Hammerstein's death, Rodgers collaborated with Stephen Sondheim, Sheldon Harnick, and Martin Charnin.

Biographer Meryle Secrest reports that Richard Rodgers was married in his wife's parents' home, not in a synagogue. His wife Dorothy said, "We are not religious. We are social Jews." Secrest continues: "Those around him knew that . . . Rodgers was an atheist. At the age of twelve [his daughter] Mary Rodgers Guettel asked her father whether he believed in God and he answered that he believed in people. 'If somebody is really sick, I don't pray to God, I look for the best doctor in town.'"

On the subject of "inspiration," Rodgers said: "That's a bad word for what happens to me when I write. What I do is not as fancy as some people may think. It is simply using the medium to express emotion.

. . . This isn't a question of sitting on the top of a hill and waiting for inspiration to strike. It's work. People have said 'You're a genius.' I say, 'No, it's my job.'"

Stephen Sondheim

(1930–) | *composer, lyricist—best known:* West Side Story, Gypsy, A Funny Thing Happened on the Way to the Forum, Sunday in the Park with George

Composer and lyricist Stephen Sondheim was born in New York City to nonreligious Jewish parents. Writes biographer Meryle Secrest,

> *The school chosen for him had been founded by Felix Adler, a nineteenth-century social reformer who had begun life as a rabbinical student but who had decided that religion was inadequate to deal with the problems of the modern world. [T]he Ethical Culture School was the ideal solution for parents uneasily poised between a strict adherence to old dogmas and atheism. Although it was considered a radical school, it might have looked to both Sondheims as the only alternative. As for religious instruction, Stephen Joshua Sondheim received none at all. He never had a bar mitzvah ceremony, he knew nothing about the observances of the Jewish calendar, and he did not enter a synagogue until he was nineteen years old.*

After his parents divorced, he moved with his mother to Pennsylvania, where their neighbor happened to be lyricist Oscar Hammerstein II. Serving as a surrogate father, Hammerstein took Stephen under his wings and inspired him to write music, critiquing his early childish work and giving him invaluable pointers. Sondheim then majored in music at Williams College. At age 25, he wrote the lyrics for the musical play *West Side Story*.

Charles Strouse

(1928–) | composer—best known: Bye Bye Birdie, Annie, *"Those Were the Days" (theme from* All in the Family*)*

Charles Strouse's songs have been performed by such stars as Barbra Streisand, Frank Sinatra, Tony Bennett, Bobby Darin, Mandy Patinkin, Harry Connick Jr., Bobby Rydell, Jay Z, Vic Damone, Louis Armstrong, Nina Simone, Grace Jones, and Duke Ellington and his Orchestra.

Strouse has written the scores to over 30 stage musicals, four Hollywood films, two orchestral works, and an opera.

Charles Strouse is not a believer. "I grudgingly went to Sunday Hebrew school," he writes in his memoirs, "but mostly, I think, we were sent just to get us out of the house. . . . We were not what you would call religious, and this has stuck with me to this day." He describes a full and purpose-filled life, working for music as well as civil rights. He traveled with actress Butterfly McQueen, a lifelong atheist, experiencing firsthand racial discrimination in the South (he was spat upon for traveling with a black woman), and marched for civil rights with Sammy Davis Jr. in Selma, Alabama, in 1965.

Annie Laurie Gaylor and I had the pleasure of interviewing Charles on Freethought Radio in 2009. "Though my father wasn't an atheist, I am," he told us. "I escaped being bar mitzvahed, but I never did escape being beat up by young kids for being Jewish." Asked when he realized he was an atheist, he said:

*My sister died in '41 of breast cancer, and I remember a
rabbi saying that "God in his infinite wisdom has chosen
to take this young girl." That was a point in my life that I
said there couldn't be any God. I understand why people
do believe in it, and frankly, I'm a little puzzled, though a
little pleased, that there is a radio program like yours that
talks about it, because as an atheist, at least my kind of
it, I don't need any persuasion. I've been persuaded for a
great number of years now, by the wars, the calamities, the
religious antagonism among people, and their stupid rules.*

Charles Strouse says he thinks the reason he wrote
so many "happy songs" is because having grown up during the Depression with a mother who was constantly depressed, optimism became his way out. "Put on a happy
face . . . The sun'll come up tomorrow," he tells us, with
no thought of an afterlife.

Biographical Sources by Subject

2000 Years = 2000 Years of Disbelief: Famous People With the Courage to Doubt, by James Haught (Prometheus Books, 1996).

BDMR = A Biographical Dictionary of Modern Rationalists, by Joseph McCabe (Watts, 1920).

WWH = Who's Who in Hell, edited by Warren Allen Smith (Barricade Books, 2000).

WWS = Women Without Superstition: "No Gods—No Masters" (The Collected Writings of Women Freethinkers of the Nineteenth and Twentieth Centuries), edited by Annie Laurie Gaylor (Freedom From Religion Foundation, Inc., 1997).

Douglas Adams
Interview, American Atheist, Winter 1998–99.

Felix Adler
Founding address of New York Society for Ethical Culture, May 15, 1876.

Edward Albee
"Who's Afraid of Virginia Woolf," 1962.

Ayaan Hirsi Ali
Infidel, 2007.

Woody Allen
"My Philosophy," The New Yorker, December 27, 1969.
Interview by Simon Hattenstone, The Guardian Weekend, March
    29, 1997, cited in *WWH*.

Natalie Angier
"But What About the Tooth Fairy, Mom? Raising a Healthy God-
    free Child in a Hopelessly God-struck Nation," acceptance speech
    of the "Emperor Has No Clothes" Award at the Freedom From
    Religion Foundation convention, reprinted in *Freethought Today*,
    November, 2003.

Philip Appleman
"Prairie Dogs," in *Karma, Dharma, Pudding & Pie,* 2009.
"In a Dark Time," *Freethought Today*, September 2006. This poem,
    set to music, was played on Freethought Radio, July 1, 2006,
    and June 2, 2007.

Isaac Asimov
Free Inquiry, Spring 1982.
As quoted in *Philosophy on the Go*, by Joey Green, 2007.
Letter, February 22, 1966.

Michelle Bachelet
"Socialist Bachelet wins Chilean presidency," *USA Today*, January
    15, 2006.

Mikhail Bakunin
"God and the State," 1883, later published in English by Emma
    Goldman's Mother Earth Publishing, 1916.

John Ballance.
From *BDMR*.

Mikhail Baryshnikov
The Larry King Show, May 5, 2002.

Charles Baudelaire
Quoted in *WWH*.

Pierre Bayle
Thoughts on the Comet, 1682.

Simone de Beauvoir
"Situation and Character," *The Second Sex*, 1949, translated and edited by II. M. Parshley, 1953.

Ludwig Van Beethoven
A Biographical Dictionary of Modern Rationalists, by Joseph Mc-Cabe, Thoemmes Continuum, 1998.
Life of Beethoven, Ludwig Nohl, Best Books, 2001.
Beethoven: Biography of a Genius, George Marek. Funk and Wagnalls, 1969.
2,000 Years of Disbelief: Famous People with the Courage to Doubt, James Haught, Prometheus Books, 1996.
Dictionary of Atheism, Skepticism, & Humanism, by Bill Cooke, Prometheus Books, 2006.

Hector Berlioz
Berlioz, Volume One: The Making of an Artist (1803–1832), by David Cairns, University of California Press, 2000.
Berlioz, Volume Two: Servitude and Greatness (1832–1869), by David Cairns, University of California Press, 2000.
Berlioz: The Man and His Work, by W. J. Turner, Vienna House, New York, 1974 (Originally published by J.M. Dent and Sons, Ltd., London, 1939).

Irving Berlin
As Thousands Cheer: The Life of Irving Berlin, by Laurence Bergreen, Da Capo Press, 1990.

Steve Benson
"From Latter-Day Saint to Latter Day Ain't," *Freethought Today*, December 1999.

Jeremy Bentham
Constitutional Code, 1830. (See also *Behold the Antichrist: Bentham on Religion,* by Delos McKown, 2004).

Ingmar Bergman
The Magic Lantern, an autobiography, 1987.

Ambrose Bierce
The Devil's Dictionary, 1906.

Georges Bizet
Bizet, by William Dean, Colier Books, 1962.

Bjornstjerne Bjornson
BDMR.

Lillie Devereux Blake
Woman's Place To-Day, 1883.

Ben Bova
Interview on *Freethought Radio*, July 18, 2009.

Paul D. Boyer
"A Path to Atheism," *Freethought Today*, March 2004.

Charles Bradlaugh
"A Plea for Atheism," *Humanity's Gain from Unbelief*, 1929.

Hypatia Bradlaugh Bonner
Motto of *Reformer*, a British journal Bonner launched in 1897.
Her final "Testament."

Johannes Brahms
Johannes Brahms: A Biography, by Jan J. Swafford, Vintage Books,
   1999.

Marlon Brando
Refusing to recite a religious oath while testifying at his son Christian's trial, 1990. *WWH*.

Georg Buchner
"Danton's Death," 1835.

Pearl Buck
"Advice to unborn novelists," 1949, cited by George Seldes, *The
   Great Quotations*.
What America Means to Me, 1947.

Luis Buñuel
Paris Notes, December 98/January 99.

Luther Burbank
Interview in *San Francisco Bulletin*, January 22, 1926.

Anthony Burgess
New York Times obituary, November 26, 1993.

Robert Burns
Letter to Robert Muir, March 8, 1788.

John Burroughs
The Light of Day, by John Burroughs, 1900.

George Carlin
Napalm and Silly Putty, 2001.

Andrew Carnegie
The Autobiography of Andrew Carnegie, 1920.
Letter to Sir James Donaldson, 1905. Letters in Library of Congress collection, cited in *Andrew Carnegie,* by Joseph Frazier Wall, 1970.
Letter to Elizabeth Haldane, 1913, Haldane Papers, National Library of Scotland, Edinburgh.

Henry Cavendish
Life of the Hon. H. Cavendish, by Dr. G. Wilson 1851, cited by *BDMR.*

Daniel Henry Chamberlain
North American Review article, reprinted in *The Freethinker,* November 15, 1908.

Charlie Chaplain
My Autobiography, 1964, cited in *WWH.*

Lydia Maria Child
The Progress of Religious Ideas Through Successive Ages, 1855.

Noam Chomsky
Chronicles of Dissent: Interviews with David Barsamian, 1992.

Arthur C. Clarke
Popular Science, August 2004.

Georges Clemenceau
"Gods and Laws," *In the Evening of My Thought,* translated by William Raymond Clark, 1929. For more about Clemenceau, see

Prof. Clark's article, "George Clemenceau: Journalist: Statesman, Atheist," *Freethought Today*, August 2002.

Voltairine de Cleyre
"Sex Slavery," essay and speech, 1895. Can be read in *Exquisite Rebel: The Essays of Voltairine de Cleyre-Feminist, Anarchist, Genius*, by Sharon Presley and Crispin Sartwell, 2005.

Jimmy Cliff
The Colbert Report, August 2, 2010.

Edward Clodd
Cited in *BDMR*.

George Clooney
Profile in *Washington Post*, September 28, 1997.

Samuel Taylor Coleridge
Letter to Thomas Allsop, c. 1820.
Ctied in *Letters, Conversations with Recollections of Samuel Taylor Coleridge,* by Thomas Allsop, 1836.

Anthony Collins
Definition of "freethought," *Discourse of Freethinking*, 1713.

Lucy Colman
Paper delivered at New York teacher's convention, printed in *The Truth Seeker*, March 5, 1887.

August Comte
The Positive Philosophy, 1853.

Marquis de Condorcet (Marie-Jean-Antoine-Nicolas Caritat)
From letter Thomas Jefferson wrote to Thomas Law, Poplar Forest, 1814.
Sketch for a Historical Picture of the Progress of the Human Mind, 1794.
The Noble Philosopher: Condorcet and the Enlightenment, by Edward Goodell, 1994.

Robin Cook

BBC News, "Mourners' funeral tribute to Cook," August 12, 2005.

Aaron Copland

"Copland and the Prophetic Voice," by Howard, Pollack. See Oja, Carol J., and Judith Tick, Judith, editors. *Aaron Copland and His World*. Princeton University Press, 2005.

Francis Crick

What Mad Pursuit: A Personal View of Scientific Discovery, 1988.

David Cronenberg

Interview, *Esquire* magazine, February 1992.

Marie Curie

What Do I Read Next?, by Marie Curie (a memoir of Pierre Curie), 1924.

Charles Darwin

Letter to Rev. J. Fordyce on July 7, 1879.

Richard Dawkins

"Time to Stand Up," written for the Freedom From Religion Foundation, September 2001. (http://www.ffrf.org/news/timely-topics/time-to-stand-up)

Eugene V. Debs

Cited in *Eugene V. Debs: A Man Unafraid*, by McAlister Coleman, 1930.

Debs describing his teenage reaction to a hellfire lecture by a priest. Cited in *Talks with Debs in Terre Haute* by David Karsner, 1922.

Cited by Herbert M. Morais and William Cahn, *Gene Debs: The Story of a Fighting American*, 1948.

Claude Debussy

Interview in *Excelsior*, February 11, 1911. As quoted in *Claude Debussy: His Life and Works*, by Léon Vallas, 1933.

Interview in *Comoedia*, printed May 18, 1911. As quoted in *Claude Debussy: His Life and Works*, by Léon Vallas, 1933.

Frederick Delius
Grieg and Delius: A Chronicle of their Friendship in Letters, edited by Lionel Carley, Rizzoli Intl, 1993.

Daniel C. Dennett
"The Bright Stuff," *New York Times*, July 12, 2003.

John Dewey
The Influence of Darwin on Philosophy, 1909.

Baron d'Holbach
Common Sense, 1772.

Denis Diderot
Addition to Philosophical Thoughts, c. 1762.

Marlene Dietrich
Cited in *Marlene Dietrich Life & Legend*, by Steven Bach, 2000.

Ani DiFranco
Interview by Matthew Rothschild, *The Progressive*, May 2000.

Ann Druyan
"Ann Druyan Talks About Science, Religion, Wonder, Awe . . . and Carl Sagan," *The Skeptical Inquirer*, November/December 2003.

W.E.B. Du Bois
The Autobiography of W.E.B. DuBois: A Soliloquy on Viewing My Life from the Last Decade of Its First Century. New York, NY: International Publishers Co. Inc., 1968.
"On Christianity," by W.E.B Du Bois, chapter in *African-American Humanism: An Anthology*, edited by Norm R. Allen, Jr.

Isadora Duncan
My Life, by Isadora Duncan, 1927.

Christopher Eccleston
"Heaven and Earth Show," BBC, April 4, 2005.

Barbara Ehrenreich
"Cultural Baggage," by Barbara Ehrenreich, *New York Times Magazine*, April 5, 1992.

Albert Einstein

Column for the *New York Times*, November 9, 1930 (reprinted in the *New York Times* obituary, April 19, 1955).

"Science, Philosophy and Religion, A Symposium," published by the Conference on Science, Philosophy and Religion in their Relation to the Democratic Way of Life, Inc., New York, 1941.

Letter to philosopher Eric Gutkind, dated January 3, 1954 (in *The Guardian*, "Childish superstition: Einstein's letter makes view of religion relatively clear," by James Randerson, May 13, 2008).

Edward Elgar

Byron Adams. "Elgar's Later Oratorios: Roman Catholicism, decadence and the Wagnerian dialectic of shame and grace" (see Grimley, Daniel).

Frances Farmer

"God Dies," award-winning essay at 16, printed in *The Scholastic*, May 2, 1931.

Jules Feiffer

Cited by *WWH*.

Richard Feynman

The Pleasure of Finding Things Out, 1981.

W.C. Fields

Cited by *WWH*.

Harvey Fierstein

In the segment "Outtakes," from the program *In the Life*, broadcast by Generation Q, November 2004.

Henry Fonda

Henry Fonda *My Life*, by Howard Teichmann, 1981.

Harrison Ford

Parade, July 7, 2002.

Jodie Foster

Interview with Dan McLeod, *The Georgia Straight*, July 10–17, 1997.

Stephen Foster

Emerson, Ken, *Doo-Dah! Stephen Foster and the Rise of American Popular Culture*. Da Capo Press, 1998.

Thanks to Fred Edwords of the American Humanist Association for additional material on Stephen Foster.

John Fowles

Quoted in *The New York Times Book Review*, May 31, 1998.

Anatole France

Letter to the Freethought Congress at Paris, 1905, cited by *BDMR*.

Sigmund Freud

The Future of an Illusion, 1927.
Moses and Monotheism, 1939.

Erich Fromm

Man for Himself, 1947.

Robert Frost

"Not All There," in *A Further Range*, 1936.

Zona Gale

Unfinished autobiography. Referenced in *WWS*.

John Galsworthy

Moods, Songs, and Doggerels, 1912.

Helen H. Gardener

Men, Women and Gods, 1885.

Giuseppe Garibaldi

Letter, 1880, cited by *BDMR*.

Janeane Garofalo

"Showbiz," August 1995.
Feel This Book: An Essential Guide to Self-Empowerment, Spiritual Supremacy, and Sexual Satisfaction by Janeane Garofalo and Ben Stiller, 1999.

William Lloyd Garrison

Remarks at the 5th national woman's rights conference in Philadelphia on October 18, 1854. *History of Woman Suffrage,* Vol. 1, pp. 382–383.

Anne Nicol Gaylor

Wording proposed to counter religious displays. Appears on annual Winter Solstice sign displayed at the Wisconsin State Capitol every December since 1996. Photo of sign in *Freethought Today,* December 2009.

Ira Gershwin and George Gershwin

Rosenberg, Deena, *Fascinating Rhythm: The Collaboration of George and Ira Gershwin.* Dutton, 1991.

Greenberg, Rodney, *George Gershwin.* Phaidon Press Limited, 1998.

Jablonski, Edward, *Gershwin: A Biography.* Doubleday, 1987.

Ricky Gervais

Inside the Actors Studio, Bravo TV, January 12, 2009.

Ella E. Gibson

The Godly Women of the Bible by an Ungodly Woman of the Nineteenth Century, 1870s.

Hermione Gingold

In her biography *How to Grow Old Disgracefully,* 1988.

Charlotte Perkins Gilman

In This Our World, 1893.

Emma Goldman

"Was My Life Worth Living?" *Harper's Monthly* magazine, December 1934.

Goldman's two essays "The Failure of Christianity," 1913, and "The Philosophy of Atheism," 1916, contain her freethought views.

1898 speech to a liberal Detroit congregation, "Living My Life," in *Living My Life,* by Emma Goldman, 1934.

Rebecca Newberger Goldstein
The Humanist, May/June 2010.

Stephen J. Gould
Interview, *Life*, December 1988.

Ulysses S. Grant
Brown's *Life of Grant*, cited by Franklin Steiner, *The Religious Beliefs of Our Presidents*.
Ulysses S. Grant, address delivered in Des Moines, Iowa, in 1875.

Alan Hale
Series of e-mails starting January 14, 1997, posted on the Secular Web Kiosk between Alan Hale and a creationist.

Edmund Halley
Biographical Dictionary, by Alexander Chalmers, 1817, cited in *BDMH*.

Frances Hamerstrom
Speech before 1986 national convention of the Freedom From Religion Foundation, reprinted in *Freethought Today*, January/February 1987.

Yip Harburg
Who Put the Rainbow in The Wizard of Oz?, by Harold Meyerson and Ernie Harburg, University of Michigan Press, 1995.
The Making of The Wizard Of Oz: Movie Magic and Studio Power in the Prime of MGM, by Aljean Harmetz, Hyperion, 1998.
Rhymes for the Irreverent, by Yip Harburg. FFRF, Inc., in collaboration with the Yip Harburg Foundation, 2006.

Stephen Hawking
Black Holes and Baby Universes and Other Essays, 1993.

Josephine K. Henry
Letter responding to Frances Willard's praise of the bible, published in the Appendix of *The Woman's Bible*, 1897.

Katharine Hepburn
Ladies Home Journal, October 1991.

Joe Hill
Desert Evening News, Utah, 1915.

Christopher Hitchens
"The Lord and the Intellectuals," *Harper's*, July 1982, cited in *2000 Years*.

Thomas Hobbes
Leviathan, 1651.

Eric Hoffer
The True Believer, 1951.

George Jacob Holyoake
The Origin and Nature of Secularism, Chapter 3, 1896.

Alice Hubbard
Introduction to *An American Bible*, 1912.

Elbert Hubbard
From *An American Bible*, edited by Alice Hubbard, 1912.

Langston Hughes
"Goodbye Christ," in "Rage, Repudiation, and Endurance: Langston Hughes's Radical Writings," *The Langston Hughes Review*, 1993.

Rupert Hughes
"Why I Quit Going to Church," Freethought Press Association, 1924.

David Hume
The Natural History of Religion, 1757.
An Enquiry Concerning Human Understanding, 1748.
Zora Neale Hurston, "Religion," from *Dust Tracks on a Road* by Zora Neale Hurston, 1942, anthologized in *African-American Humanism: An Anthology,* edited by Norm R. Allen Jr., 1991.

Julian Huxley
Religion Without Revelation, 1927, revised 1956.

Henrik Ibsen
Letter to Georg Brandes, quoted in *Ibsen* by Anathon Aall (*Henrik Ibsen Als Dichter Und Denker*), 1906.

Eddie Izzard
"I Believe That Eddie Izzard Is Our Future," interview by Ali MacLean, *Huffington Post*, August 16, 2010.

Elton John
Observer Music Monthly magazine in an interview with Scissor Sisters's Jake Shears, November 2006.

Sonia Johnson
1982 speech before the Freedom From Religion Foundation, Madison, Wisconsin.

Angelina Jolie
The Onion, "A.V. Club," September 7–13, 2000.

John Keats
"Sonnet Written in Disgust of Vulgar Superstition," 1816.

Ludovic Kennedy
"Put away childish things," *The Guardian* (UK), April 17, 2003.

Jerome Kern
Jerome Kern: A Biography, by Michael Freedland, Stein and Day, 1981.

Michael Kinsley
"The Religious Superiority Complex: It's OK to think your God's the greatest, but you don't have to rub it in," *Time* magazine, November 3, 2003.

Margaret Knight
Morals Without Religion, 1955.

Harold Walter Kroto
From his Nobel Prize autobiography, 1996.

Stanley Kubrick
Interview, *American Cinematographer*, 1963.

Milan Kundera
Interview with Olga Carlisle, *New York Times*, May 19, 1985.

Burt Lancaster
Burt Lancaster: An American Life, by Kate Buford, 2000.

Burton Lane
Freethought Radio, produced by the Freedom From Religion Foundation. Archives at http://ffrf.org/news/radio. Interview with Lynn Lane, December 19, 2009.

Burton Lane
Harburg, Yip. *The Yip Harburg Songbook*. Warner Brothers Publications, 1994.

Cloris Leachman
Interview by Cal Fussman in *Esquire*, January, 2009.

Ursula K. LeGuin
Introduction to *The Left Hand of Darkness*, 1969.
"Look! There Is No Emperor!" acceptance speech for the Emperor Has No Clothes award, reprinted in *Freethought Today*, December 2009.

Tom Lehrer
Telephone interview with Jeremy Mazner, November 21, 1995, in *Tom Lehrer: The Political Musician That Wasn't*, by Jeremy Mazner, 1997.
"Vatican Rag." A version of this song can be heard on the Freedom From Religion Foundation CD *Friendly Neighborhood Atheist*.

John Lennon
Playboy, January, 1981.

Sinclair Lewis
Quoted by Will Durant in *On the Meaning of Life*, 1932.

Jack London
Cited *WWH*.

Henry Wadsworth Longfellow
Friend W. D. Howells, writing about Longfellow in *Literary Friends and Acquaintances*, 1901. Cited in *BDMR*.

Amy Lowell
"What's O'Clock," 1925.

James Russell Lowell
Literary Essays, Witchcraft, Vol. II, 1891.

Rosa Luxemburg
"Socialism and the Churches," 1905, first published by the Polish
Social Democratic Party.

Andre Malraux
Cited in *WWH*.

Karl Marx
Portraits from Memory, by Bertrand Russell, 1956.
A Criticism of the Hegelian Philosophy of Right, 1844.

Abraham H. Maslow
Description of Maslow's views by Richard J. Lowery, *A. H. Maslow:
An Intellectual Portrait*, 1974.

Henri Matisse
The Unknown Matisse, by Henry Spurling, 1998.
Cited in *WWH*. (This quote is similar to Neitzsche's, "I would only
believe in a God who knew how to dance," in *Thus Spoke Zarath-
rustra*, 1883).

Ian McEwan
Interview, NPR affiliate KUSP, Capitola, California, February 16,
1998.

Butterfly McQueen
Atlanta Journal and Constitution, October 8, 1989. The quote
about slavery was made into a billboard and bus sign by the Freedom From Religion Foundation and displayed around the country.
See *Freethought Today*, March 2009.

H. L. Mencken
A Mencken Chrestomathy, 1949.
New York Times Magazine, September 11, 1955.
A Mencken Chrestomathy, 1949.
A Book of Burlesques 1916, 1924.

A *Mencken Chrestomathy*, 1949.
"Mencken's Creed," cited in *Great Thoughts, Revised and Updated*, by George Seldes, 1996.

George Meredith
Letter to Mr. Clodd (Memories), cited by *BDMR*.
Fortnightly Review, July 1909.

James Michener
Interview, *Parade* magazine, November 24, 1991, cited in *WWH*. (A similar passage is found in *The World Is My Home* by Robert Michener, 1991.)

John Stuart Mill
Autobiography, 1873.

A. A. Milne
Cited in *2000 Years*.

Moliere
Monologue by Cleante, *Tartuffe*, 1667.

Robin Morgan
"Fighting Words for a Secular America," *Ms.* magazine, Fall 2004.

Wolfgang Amadeus Mozart
Ulibichev, A., *Mozart's Leben,* 1847.

Fridtjof Nansen
"Science and the Purpose of Life." Speech published by the Rationalist Press Association, 1909. Cited in *BDMR*.

Paul Newman
Paul Newman: A Life, by Shawn Levy, 2009.
According to *WWH*, Newman once told TV interviewer Barbara Walters that he didn't believe in an afterlife.

Jack Nicholson
AARP magazine, March/April 2008.

Leslie Nielsen
Esquire magazine interview, April 2008.

Friedrich Nietzsche
Human, All-Too-Human, 1878.
Why I Am a Destiny, 1888.

Culbert Olson
"Hell" quote from genealogytrails.com/cal/government.html.
Quoted in SFGate.com, September 18, 2005, by Bill Whalen.
"Address of the Hon. Culbert L. Olson to the 1956 Annual Conven-
tion of the United Secularists of America," *Progressive World,*
October 1956.

Eugene O'Neill
Instructions to his wife, quoted in *O'Neill, Son and Artist,* by Louis
Shaeffer, 1968.

George Orwell
Essay "Reflections on Gandhi," 1949. Printed in *The Orwell
Reader,* edited by Richard H. Rovere, 1961.

Robert Owen
*Evidences of Christianity: A Debate with Alexander Campbell and
Robert Owen,* 1829.
Essays on the Principle of the Formation of Human Character, 1816.
Autobiography, *Threading My Way,* 1874.

Niccolò Paganini
Conestabile, Giovanni Carlo della Staffa, *Vita di Niccolò Paganini da
Genova,* 1851.

Linus Pauling
"Scientist for the Ages" (oregonstate.edu).

Joaquin Phoenix
Nylon Guys magazine, Winter, 2008.
Sunday Times (UK), April, 1999.

Brad Pitt
In an interview with Ann Curry on *The Today Show,* August 13,
2009.
Parade magazine, 2007.

Edgar Allan Poe
"Eureka," 1848.

Katha Pollitt
"Is Atheism the New Black?" speech to the Freedom From Religion Foundation Convention in 2007, reprinted in *Freethought Today*, March 2008.

Cole Porter
McBrien, William, *Cole Porter*. Vintage Books, 1998.

Natalie Portman
Rolling Stone, "The Private Life of Natalie Portman," by Chris Heath, June 20, 2002.

Sergei Prokovfiev
Robinson, Harlow, *Sergei Prokofiev: A Biography*. Northeastern University Press, 1987.

Marcel Proust
Remembrance of Things Past (1913–26), cited in *The Great Thoughts*, edited by George Seldes.

Samuel Porter Putnam
My Religious Experience, 1891.

Daniel Radcliffe
Quoted in "Daniel Radcliffe: a cool nerd," by Anita Singh, *The Telegraph* (UK), July 4, 2009.

Ayn Rand
Character John Galt in *Atlas Shrugged*, 1957.

Tony Randall
Washington Post, September 25, 2003.

David Randolph
This Is Music: A Guide To The Pleasures of Listening. Creative Arts Books, 1994. (Originally McGraw Hill, 1964.) Available from The Mastrerwork and Art Foundation, Whippany, New Jersey.

SE THE GOOD ATHEIST

Ron Reagan
"One Boy's Journey to Godlessness," acceptance speech for the
Emperor Has No Clothes Award at the Freedom From Religion
Foundation annual convention, November, 2009. Reprinted in
Freethought Today, March, 2010.

Marilla M. Ricker
"Science Against Creeds," *I Am Not Afraid Are You?*, 1917.

J. M. Robertson
Pagan Christs, 1903.

Richard Rodgers
Secrest, Meryle, *Somewhere For Me: A Biography of Richard
Rodgers*. Applause, 2001.

Auguste Rodin
Auguste Rodin, Camille Mauclair (English translation, 1905).

Carl Rogers
New York Times obituary article, February 6, 1987.

Andy Rooney
Sincerely, Andy Rooney, 1999.

Maurice Ravel
Orenstein, Arbie, editor, *Ravel: Man and Musician*. Dover, 1991.

Giochino Rossini
Servadio, Gaia, *Rossini*. Carroll & Graf Publishers, 2003.

Philip Roth
Interviewed by Rita Braver on *CBS Sunday Morning*, October 3,
2010.

Jean Jacques Rousseau
The Social Contract, 1762.

Jane Rule
*Brave Souls: Writers and Artists Wrestle with God, Love, Death and
the Things that Matter,* by Douglas Todd, 1996.

Salman Rushdie
"Slaughter in the Name of God," *Washington Post*, March 8, 2002.

Bertrand Russell
"The Faith of a Rationalist," broadcast by the BBC in 1953.
"What I Believe," 1925, reprinted in *Why I Am Not a Christian*, 1957.

Oliver Sacks
Uncle Tungsten, pp. 178–79, 2001.
"The Invasion of Irrationalism," acceptance speech, *Freethought Today*, June/July 2006.

Carl Sagan
"The Fine Art of Baloney Detection," from *The Demon-Haunted World: Science As A Candle In The Dark*, 1996.
Billions and Billions: Thoughts on Life and Death at the Brink of the Millennium, 1997.

George Santayana
"Christian Morality," *Little Essays*, #107, 1920 (drawn from the writings of George Santayana by Logan Pearsall Smith, with the collaboration of the author).

Robert Sapolsky
"Belief and Biology," acceptance speech for the "Emperor Has No Clothes Award" at the Freedom From Religion Foundation convention in San Diego on November 23, 2003. Reprinted in *Freethought Today*, April 2003.

Jean-Paul Sartre
The Words, 1964.
Life magazine, November 6, 1964 (cited in *2000 Years*).

Ellery Schempp
"A Champion of the First Amendment," acceptance speech to FFRF, October 13, 2007, reprinted in *Freethought Today*, November 2007.

Arthur Schopenhauer
The World as Will and Idea, 1819.

Robert Schumann
Swafford, Jan, *Johannes Brahms: A Biography*. Vintage Books, 1999.

George Seldes
Witness to a Century: Encounters with the Noted, the Notorious, and the Three SOBs, 1987.

George Bernard Shaw
"Androcles and the Lion," 1912.
"Back to Methuselah," 1924.
"Preface to Androcles and the Lion," 1912.

Percy Bysshe Shelley
The Necessity of Atheism, 1811.

Upton Sinclair
Upton Sinclair's Magazine, April 1918.

Peter Singer
Project Syndicate, "Godless Morality," by Peter Singer and Marc Hauser, January 2006.
Acceptance speech for "Emperor Has No Clothes" award at the 2004 convention of the Freedom From Religion Foundation, reprinted in *Freethought Today*, May 2005.

B. F. Skinner
Brief autobiography written for *A History of Psychology in Autobiography*, by E. G. Boring and G. Lindzey, 1967.

Elmina D. Slenker
Studying the Bible, 1870.

Kay Nolte Smith
"Truth or Consequences," speech to the Freedom From Religion Foundation 1983 national convention, quoted in *WWS*.

William Smith
The Map That Changed the World, by Simon Winchester, 2002.

Barbara Smoker
"So You Believe in God!" 1974 pamphlet. Quoted in *WWS*.

Steven Soderbergh
In answer to a question posed by the "A.V. Club" section of *The Onion* newspaper, September 7–13, 2000.

Stephen Sondheim
Stephen Sondheim: A Life, by Meryle Secrest, Delta, 1998.

Edward Sorel
The Atlantic, November 6, 1997.
Lincoln Center Theater Review, "Memories of Three Left-Wing Cartoonists," Spring 2003.

Herbert Spencer
First Principles, 1862.

Benedict Spinoza
Great Thoughts, edited by George Seldes, c. 1670.
Ethics, 1677.

Elizabeth Cady Stanton
"The Degraded Status of Woman in the Bible," 1896.
An interview with the Chicago Record, June 29, 1897.

Victor J. Stenger
The New Atheism: Taking a Stand for Science and Reason, 2009.

Rod Steiger
Playboy magazine, July 1969.

John Steinbeck
Cited in *WWH*.
Nobel Prize for Literature acceptance speech, 1962.

Gloria Steinem
Interview with Annie Laurie Gaylor, *The Feminist Connection*, November 1980 (Madison, Wisconsin).

Robert Louis Stevenson
R.L.S., by Francis Watt, 1913.

Sting
Berklee College of Music commencement address in Boston, May 15, 1994.

Robert Stout
Inaugural address as president of Dunedin Freethought Association, 1880.

Richard Strauss
Ross, Alex, "The Last Emperor: Richard Strauss," *The New Yorker,* December.
Kennedy, Michael, *Richard Strauss: Man, Musician, Enigma.* Cambridge University Press, 1999.

Meryl Streep
"Meryl Streep: mother superior," by Mick Brown, *London Telegraph*, December 4, 2008.
"Movies, marriage, and turning sixty," *The Independent* (UK), January 24, 2009.

Charles Strouse
Put On a Happy Face: A Broadway Memoir. Union Square Press, 2008.
Freethought Radio, produced by the Freedom From Religion Foundation. Archives at http://ffrf.org/news/radio. Interview with Charles Strouse, June 20, 2009.

Julia Sweeney
Speech to the Freedom From Religion Foundation, October 2007. Reprinted in *Freethought Today*, December 2007.
Quote submitted by Julia Sweeney for FFRF's "Freethought of the Day."

Algernon Charles Swinburne
"Atalanta in Calydon," 1865.
Mentioned in *BDMR*.
"Hertha," 1871.
"Hymn of Man," 1871.

Thomas Szasz
The Second Sin, by Thomas Szasz, 1973.

Studs Terkel
Interview with Krista Tippett on "Speaking of Faith," American Public Media, 2004.

Emma Thompson
"Acting on outspoken beliefs," by Jane Cornwell in the *Australian*, October 15, 2008.

Henry David Thoreau
On the Duty of Civil Disobedience, 1849.
Church quote cited by *2000 Years.*

James Thurber
James Thurber: His Life and Times, by Harrison Kinney.

Joseph Turner
Life of J.M.W. Turner, Walter Thornbury, 1862, Volume 2.
Life of Turner, P.G. Hamerton, 1879.
BDMR.

Mark Twain
1904 "War Prayer." An excerpt set to music can be heard on the "Beware of Dogma" CD, produced by the Freedom From Religion Foundation.
Mark Twain's Notebooks and Journals, Notebook 27, August 1887– July 1888, edited by Frederick Anderson (1979). Cited by *2000 Years.*

Eddie Vedder
Interview with Janeane Garofalo in *CMJ New Music Report*, March 23, 1998.

Jesse Ventura
"Despite court decision, National Day of Prayer will endure in Minnesota," by Andy Birkey, April 20, 2010.
Playboy magazine, November 1999.

Giuseppe Verdi
Phillips-Matz, Mary Jane, *Verdi: A Biography.* Oxford University Press, 1993.

Gore Vidal
Letter to Warren Allen Smith, 1954, cited in *WWH.*
Time magazine, September 28, 1952.

Voltaire

John Morley, *Critical Miscellanies*, 1872, and *Bartlett's Familiar Quotations*, 10th Edition.

"Poème sur le désastre de Lisbonne" ("Poem on the Lisbon Disaster"), 1755.

Philosophical Dictionary, 1764.

Kurt Vonnegut Jr.

Fates Worse Than Death: An Autobiographical Collage of the 1980s, 1991.

Alice Walker

"The Only Reason You Want to Go to Heaven Is That You Have Been Driven Out of Your Mind," *Anything We Love Can Be Saved: A Writer's Activism*, 1998.

Barbara G. Walker

"The Skeptical Feminist," acceptance speech for the "1993 Humanist Heroine" award by the Feminist Caucus of the American Humanist Association.

James D. Watson

Youngstown State University speech, *The Vindicator*, December 2, 2003.

London Telegraph, March 22, 2003.

Beatrice Webb

H. G. Wells commenting on the Webbs, quoted in Margaret Drabble, ed., *Oxford Companion to English Literature*, 1995.

Beatrice Webb, quoted in *100 Years of Freethought*, by David Tribe, 1967.

Sidney Webb

"The Historic Basis of Socialism" (1889), cited in *Fabian Essays in Socialism*, edited by George Bernard Shaw, 1891.

Steven Weinberg

Talk given at the Conference on Cosmic Design of the American Association for the Advancement of Science in Washington, D.C., April 1999.

H. G. Wells
Experiment in Autobiography, 1934, cited in *What Great Men Think of Religion*, by Ira D. Cardiff, 1945.

Ella Wheeler Wilcox
"The World's Need," from *Custer and Other Poems*, 1896. (This poem can be heard set to music on the Freedom From Religion Foundation CD "Friendly Neighborhood Atheist.")

Oscar Wilde
The Critic as Artist, 1891.
Phrases and Philosophies for the Use of the Young, 1894.

Ralph Vaughan Williams.
R.V. W.: A Biography of Ralph Vaughan Williams by Ursula Vaughan Williams, Oxford University Press, 1988.

Bruce Willis
Interview, *George* magazine, July 1998.

Virginia Woolf
From her journal, cited by William Safire in the *New York Times*, January 10, 2005, and cited by *WWH*.

Emile Zola, "J'Accuse!"
L'Aurore, January 13, 1898.

Additional Sources

Barrett, Mary Ellin. *Irving Berlin: A Daughter's Memoir*. Limelight Editions, 1994.

Bergreen, Laurence. *As Thousands Cheer: The Life of Irving Berlin*. Da Capo Press, 1990.

Berlin, Edward A. *King of Ragtime: Scott Joplin and His Era*. Oxford University Press, 1994.

Botstein, Leon. "Copland Reconfigured." See Oja, Carol J., and Tick, Judith, editors, *Aaron Copland and His World*. Princeton University Press, 2005.

Catton, Bruce. "He Wanted to Murder the Bugler," *American Heritage,* August 1967.

Copland, Aaron. "A Modernist Defends Modern Music," *New York Times,* December 25, 1949.

Eells, George. *The Life That Late He Lived.* G. P. Putnam's Sons, 1967.

Eliscu, Edward. *With or Without a Song: A Memoir.* David Elescu, editor. Scarecrow Press, 2001.

Fenby, Eric. *Delius As I Knew Him.* Dover Publications, Inc., 1981.

Forbes, Elliot, editor. *Thayer's Life of Beethoven (Volumes I & II).* Princeton University Press, 1967.

Fordin, Hugh. *Getting to Know Him: A Biography of Oscar Hammerstein II.* Random House, 1977.

Furia, Philip. *Ira Gershwin: The Art of the Lyricist.* Oxford University Press, 1996.

Furia, Philip. *Skylark: The Life and Times of Johnny Mercer.* St. Martin's Press, 2003.

Furia, Philip. *The Poets of Tin Pan Alley: A History of America's Great Lyricists.* Oxford University Press, 1992.

Gershwin, Ira. *Lyrics on Several Occasions.* Limelight Editions, 1997.

Gorney, Sondra. *Brother, Can You Spare a Dime?: The Life of Composer Jay Gorney.* Scarecrow Press, 2005.

Grimley, Daniel and Julian Ruston, editors. *The Cambridge Companion to Elgar.* Cambridge University Press, 2004.

Holoman, D. Kern. *Berlioz.* Harvard University Press, Cambridge, Mass., 1989.

Ingersoll, Robert G. "Declaration of the Free." *The Works of Robert G. Ingersoll, Volume IV.* Dresden, 1901. Pages 415–19.

Jablonski, Edward. *Alan Jay Lerner: A Biography.* Henry Holt and Company, 1996.

Jablonski, Edward. *Harold Arlen: Rhythm, Rainbows, and Blues.* Northeastern University Press, 1996.

Jablonski, Edward. *Irving Berlin: American Troubadour.* Henry Holt and Company, 1999.

Jahoda, Gloria. *The Road to Samarkand: Frederick Delius and His Music.* Scribner's Sons, 1969.

Latham, Alison, editor. *The Oxford Companion to Music.* Oxford University Press, 2003.

MacArthur, John. "Slaves For Christ," Bible Bulletin Board, 2007, http://www.biblebb.com/files/MAC/80-321.htm.

MacFarren, Sir George. *Imperial Dictionary of Universal Biography.* W. MacKenzie. 1864.

Mancini, Henry, with Gene Lees. *Did They Mention the Music?: The Autobiography of Henry Mancini.* Cooper Square Press, 2001.

Naipaul, V.S. "Two Worlds." *Nobel Lectures: From the Literature Laureates, 1986–2006.* The New Press, 2007.

Nolan, Frederick. *Lorenz Hart: A Poet on Broadway.* Oxford University Press, 1994.

Oja, Carol J., and Judith Tick, editors. *Aaron Copland and His World.* Princeton University Press, 2005.

Price, Robert M. *Reason Driven Life: What Am I Here on Earth For?* Prometheus Books, 2006.

Rediker, Marcus. *The Slave Ship: A Human History.* Penguin, 2007.

Rodgers, Richard. *Musical Stages: An Autobiography,* Richard Rodgers Centennial Edition. Da Capo Press, 2002.

Smith, Warren Allen, *Who's Who in Hell.* Barricade Books, 2000.

Songwriters Hall of Fame, http://www.songwritershalloffame.org.

Sudhalter, Richard M., *Stardust Melody: The Life and Music of Hoagy Carmichael.* Oxford University Press, 2002.

Taylor, Theodore. *Jule: The Story of Composer Jule Styne.* Random House, 1979.

Warren, Rick. *The Purpose Driven Life: What on Earth Am I Here For?* Zondervan, 2002.

Warren, Rick. *What on Earth Am I Here For?* Zondervan, 2004.

Wiener, Jon. "Rick Warren's Clout." *The Nation,* February 2, 2009.

Winer, Deborah Grace, *On the Sunny Side of the Street: The Life and Lyrics of Dorothy Fields.* Schirmer Books, 1997.

Acknowledgments

This book owes a huge debt to the careful reading, editorial comments, and input of Annie Laurie Gaylor and Richard Harris, as well as proofing, discussion of ideas, and suggestions from Darrell Barker, Steve Hurlin, Buzz Kemper, Scott Colson, Sabrina Gaylor, Michelle DuVall, Fred Edwords, Ernie Harburg, Lynn Lane, Mary Ellin Barrett, Frank Huitt, Russ Kick, John Lombardo, Nick Markovich, David Randolph, Phyllis Rose, and John Widdicombe.

Part 2, "Profiles in Nonbelief," would not have been possible without Annie Laurie Gaylor, who wrote most of the hundreds of biographical entries for "Freethought of the Day" at the Freedom From Religion Foundation's website. Her assistant, Bonnie Gutsch, also wrote dozens of those entries. *Freethought Today* editor Bill Dunn and Jane Esbensen also contributed some of those names. I added a few more individuals who do not (yet) appear in Freethought of the Day, then I condensed data from those bios, sometimes expanding them with additional detail. Annie Laurie's book, *Women Without Superstition: "No Gods—No Masters," The Collected Writings of Women Freethinkers of the Nineteenth and Twentieth Cen-*

turies, is the main source for information on more than 50 female freethinkers. Another very useful reference is Warren Allen Smith's tome, *Who's Who in Hell: A Handbook and International Directory for Humanists, Freethinkers, Naturalists, Rationalists, and Non-Theists,* as is *A Biographical Dictionary of Modern Rationalists* by Joseph McCabe.

Index of Personal Names

Index

About the Author

Dan Barker, author of *Godless: How an Evangelical Preacher Became One of America's Leading Atheists*, is a former minister and Christian songwriter who renounced all religion after 19 years misspent "serving god." Today he fights for the separation of church and state as the co-president of the Freedom From Religion Foundation and as the host of Freethought Radio, a weekly atheist radio program broadcast daily and podcast through the natural cosmos. He plays jazz piano and lives in Madison, Wisconsin. He is married to Annie Laurie Gaylor, who is Foundation co-president and co-host of Freethought Radio.